本成果受到浙江海洋大学外国语学院学科建设经费资助,在此致谢

真实环境促进英语阅读能力发展研究

A Study of an Authentic Environment Promoting the Development of English Reading Ability

刘娜◎著

浙江工商大学出版社
ZHEJIANG GONGSHANG UNIVERSITY PRESS
·杭州·

图书在版编目(CIP)数据

真实环境促进英语阅读能力发展研究 / 刘娜著. —
杭州:浙江工商大学出版社,2023.11
ISBN 978-7-5178-5536-1

Ⅰ.①真… Ⅱ.①刘… Ⅲ.①英语—阅读教学—教学
研究—高等学校 Ⅳ.①H319.37

中国国家版本馆 CIP 数据核字(2023)第118707号

真实环境促进英语阅读能力发展研究

ZHENSHI HUANJING CUJIN YINGYU YUEDU NENGLI FAZHAN YANJIU

刘娜　著

责任编辑	张莉娅
责任校对	王　英
封面设计	望宸文化
责任印制	包建辉
出版发行	浙江工商大学出版社
	(杭州市教工路198号　邮政编码310012)
	(E-mail:zjgsupress@163.com)
	(网址:http://www.zjgsupress.com)
	电话:0571-88904980,88831806(传真)
排　　版	杭州朝曦图文设计有限公司
印　　刷	杭州宏雅印刷有限公司
开　　本	710mm×1000mm　1/16
印　　张	9.75
字　　数	200千
版 印 次	2023年11月第1版　2023年11月第1次印刷
书　　号	ISBN 978-7-5178-5536-1
定　　价	65.00元

DEDICATION

To Yaning, Audrey and Tracy

ACKNOWLEDGEMENTS

I would like to acknowledge Dr. Kristen Perry for her guidance, wisdom, and encouragement. I would also like to acknowledge Dr. Janice Almasi, Dr. Susan Cantrell, and Dr. Jungmin Lee for their contributions of time, teaching, and feedback. I am so grateful to them all for helping me through this challenging period of my life.

I would like to especially thank my husband Li Yaning and my daughters Audrey and Tracy for seeing me through this period. I am extremely grateful to all my family members and friends for their support in their own special way.

KEY CONCEPTS

Reading Comprehension

It refers to a process of constructing meaning "through interaction and involvement with written language" (Snow & Sweet, 2003, p. 10).

Academic Literacy

It refers to "being proficient in reading and writing about academic subjects" (Neeley, 2005).

English Learners (ELs)

Learners whose native language is other than English, including English as a Second Language (ESL) learners and English as a Foreign Language (EFL) learners (Calderón et al., 2011).

First Language (L1)

In this study, L1 refers to the student's native language.

Second Language (L2)

In this study, L2 is used to identify any language after the first language (Ellis, 2015).

Second Language Acquisition (SLA)

It refers to "learning of another language in a context in which the language is used as a means of wider communication" (Ellis, 2015, p. 6).

Informal Reading Inventories (IRIs)

It refers to "the individual administrated diagnostic assessments constructed to evaluate a student's strengths and weaknesses in reading performance" (Nilsson, 2008).

CONTENTS ▶▶

LIST OF TABLES ▶▶

Chapter 1 Introduction

1.1 Problem

Since President Richard Nixon visited China in 1972, Chinese students have been going to the U.S. for their studies (Chu, 2004). In 1979, the People's Republic of China and the United States announced the establishment of diplomatic relations and more Chinese students flocked into U.S. colleges or universities (Chu, 2004). From 2000 to 2012, the number of Chinese international students in the U.S. increased rapidly due to China's economic growth (Ruiz, 2014). More Chinese parents had enough money to send their children to study abroad (Ruiz, 2014). In the 2019–2020 academic year, 373,000 students from China enrolled in American higher education, accounting for roughly 34.6% of all foreign students in the U.S. (Institute of International Education [IIE], 2020). Therefore, Chinese students represented "the largest group of international students from a single country" (Liu, 2016, p. 2).

Most Chinese students are considered English Learners (ELs), but some students may have high English proficiency, particularly if they have spent long periods in English-speaking countries. International students usually face cultural and language barriers that impede their academic achievement (Smith,

2007). Compared with other international students, Chinese international students were likely to show lower English proficiency (Li et al., 2010). These Chinese college ELs faced numerous barriers to academic success such as English deficiencies, ineffective interaction with American faculty members, lack of academic English writing ability, and challenges in social communication with their peers who were proficient speakers of English (Yan & Berliner, 2009; Li et al., 2010).

Ching et al. (2017) offered a comprehensive description of the challenges that influenced Chinese international students' study and life in U.S. universities. These included the following: (1) cultural distance; (2) cultural shock; (3) social support; (4) stress and anxiety; (5) language barriers, and (6) classroom transition (Ching et al., 2017). Among these barriers, language issues directly affected students' reading comprehension, whereas others affected the affective aspects of learning and learners' comprehension and learning. Reading comprehension deserves a mention as a fundamental element of academic achievement (August et al., 2006; Taub & Benson, 2013).

However, little research has explored Chinese international students' academic English reading comprehension. To fill the gap in the literature, the purpose of this study was to describe and understand how Chinese students' perception of exposure to the authentic English-speaking environment contributed to their development of academic English reading comprehension. The following questions guided the study:

(1) What perception did Chinese international students have about their English reading comprehension in academic literacy when they were first exposed to the authentic English-speaking environment?

(2) How does Chinese international students' initial perception change

after years of exposure to the authentic English-speaking environment?

(3) How does Chinese international students' self-perception of their English reading comprehension relate to their actual reading comprehension performance?

(4) How do Chinese international students perceive the English-speaking environment contributes to their development of academic reading comprehension?

1.2 Rationale

English Learners (ELs) are defined as learners whose native language is other than English, including English as a Second Language (ESL) learners and English as a Foreign Language (EFL) learners (Calderón et al., 2011). Native language refers to the student's First Language (L1). The distinction between ESL and EFL is the native language of the country in which instruction is being provided. An ESL context is one where English is the predominant national language and is spoken outside the classroom. By contrast, an EFL context describes a context where English is not the native language and is spoken only in the classroom (Calderón et al., 2011).

It is important to consider the distinction between ESL and EFL. There are two main differences. First, ESL is more immersive, and students experience a greater level of exposure, which results in much more "input and interaction" (Ellis, 2015, p. 12). The second difference is the cultural aspect. Students in an ESL context can easily apply what they have learned to real-life situations (Brown, 1994).

Identifying the distinction can offer implications for teaching and help students learn English efficiently. Typically, Chinese students are EFL learners before going to study in the U.S. as they have learned English in China. But after going to the U.S., they become ESL learners since the U.S. is an English-speaking country.

In the U.S. ELs are classified into foreign-born ELs (immigrants, refugees, and asylees from non-English speaking contexts), U.S.-born ELs (the children of non-English-speaking immigrants, refugees, or asylees), and non-English-speaking international students and their families (Wrigley et al., 2009). These international students comprise K-12 students and college students. Non-English-speaking international college students are college ELs attending undergraduate and graduate programs whose native language is other than English.

Moreover, college ELs consist of immigrant college ELs and nonimmigrant college ELs (Stebleton, 2011). Compared with immigrant college ELs, nonimmigrant international college students face diverse limitations based on their student visas.

Generally, the U.S. Department of State Travel requires that a citizen of a foreign country who wishes to study in the U.S. must obtain one of three types of student visas including F-1, M-1, and J-1. The F-1 visa is issued to students who attend a full-time degree or academic program at a school, college, or university. A student with a M-1 visa is allowed to complete his/her full-time non-academic or vocational study. The J-1 visa is for nonimmigrant individuals approved to participate in work-and study-based exchange visitor programs.

However, the three types of student visas have various restrictions. For example, a student with a F-1 visa may not work legally off-campus without special permission and his/her dependents are not allowed to work in the U.S. (Galstyan, 2020). M-1 students may not work full-time out of campus and may not continue higher education in the U. S to get their degrees (Visa Guide World, 2020). A J-1 holder has a two-year mandatory home residency requirement (Simple Citizen, 2020). With these visa restrictions, students might not be able to complete their programs efficiently since international tuition is expensive and work opportunities are limited or forbidden. If a student fails academically, his/her student visa would be revoked (Ford, 2020).

Among these nonimmigrant college ELs, Chinese international students compose the largest group of international students in the U. S. The international center of a university in the mid-South (2020) showed there were 462 Chinese international undergraduate and graduate students enrolled in Spring 2020, accounting for roughly 30% of all foreign students. As ELs, Chinese international students face multitudinous challenges in academic contexts even though they have all passed the Test of English as a Foreign Language (TOEFL) and the International English Language Testing System (IELTS) and have met the English language proficiency requirements for admission to the U.S. institutions of higher education.

The TOEFL and IELTS are two major assessments for identifying international college ELs' English proficiency for academic admission to colleges and universities in the U.S., Canada, and other parts of the world. The TOEFL offers both an Internet-based Test (iBT) and a Paper-delivered Test (PDT). The TOEFL iBT is more common and comprises four sections: listening, reading, speaking, and writing (Matthiesen, 2011). Based on a *U. S. News* article, the average minimum TOEFL iBT score for U. S. universities is 78 (Ross, 2017).

Likewise, the IELTS has two modules—academic and general, and each module consists of four sections: reading, writing, listening, and speaking. The

academic module is widely used for entry into colleges or universities. An
IELTS score of between 6.0 and 7.0 in the academic component illustrates
international students' English proficiency for admission (Feast, 2002). For
instance, the International Center of the University of Kentucky requires the
minimum acceptable score of 71 on the TOEFL iBT or 6.0 on the IELTS for
undergraduate admissions, and 79 on the TOEFL iBT or 6.5 on the IELTS for
graduate admissions. The TOEFL and IELTS examine students' general reading
abilities, but they are not necessarily reading comprehension assessments.
Besides, if a student meets the minimum score, it does not mean that he/she
has the language competency to be successful in a particular academic
discipline.

Lei et al. (2010) stated that ELs faced numerous barriers in academic
literacy at the college level. Academic literacy can be defined as being
proficient in reading and writing about academic subjects (Neeley, 2005). It is
also a generic ability to be developed in academic contexts for students (Read,
2015). Academic literacy includes reading, writing, discourse for school, and
knowledge of multiple genres of text (Short & Fitzsimmons, 2007). It plays a
crucial role in students' academic achievement. Curry (2004) also described
that learning academic literacy was a challenge for ELs which involved
engaging in a variety of academic social practices and negotiating multiple
academic discourses in various circumstances. For example, a student majoring
in history would need to have very different language competencies than
someone majoring in engineering. The academic language demands of these
disciplines vary dramatically.

Reading comprehension, a process to extract and construct meaning by
interacting with written language (RAND Reading Study Group & Snow,

2002), is the most important component of academic literacy (August et al., 2006). It is a critical skill for native speakers and ELs in academic contexts (Kern, 1988), even for college academic success (Taub & Benson, 2013). International college students typically have smaller vocabularies, less background knowledge of the texts, and less familiarity with mainstream discourse patterns than their native English-speaking peers (August et al., 2006). Consequently, they perform more poorly on tests of reading comprehension than their English-speaking peers (Hendricks, 2013). However, we still do not know much about differences in reading comprehension across language groups. There is no data to show how speakers of different languages such as Spanish, Arabic, and Chinese compare to each other.

Reading comprehension for international college ELs can directly influence their academic achievement. Generally, reading comprehension is measured by a series of questions or by a cloze task (Nag, 2017b; Zuilkowski et al., 2019). Less commonly, it is assessed by sentence-based tasks (Laws et al., 2016; Leider et al., 2013; Leikin & Assayag Bouskila, 2004). A reading comprehension assessment typically involves reading a passage, retelling the text, and answering a series of questions (Nag, 2017b).

There are some issues in comprehension assessments for different groups of learners. For instance, some work examined a few adult learners and found that they were struggling to bridge the gap between common life knowledge and college knowledge (Graham et al., 2000; Murphy & Fleming, 2000; Ross-Gordon, 2003). For ELs, researchers focused more on K-12 students' reading comprehension progress rather than on college students' (de Jong & van der Leij, 2003; Thorndike, 1973; Torgesen et al., 1997; Mokhtari & Niederhauser, 2013; Uccelli et al., 2015). For adult/college ELs, comprehension assessment studies emphasized general college ELs instead of identifying the different language subgroup students such as Chinese, Arabic, or Spanish in the ESL context (Hendricks, 2013; Diaz, 2018; Zhang, 1992). Usually, a reading comprehension assessment happens for college ELs at their initial admission when they take the TOEFL or IELTS. Currently, there is a dearth of studies that model college ELs' development of reading comprehension over time (e.g. both when they started to study and after they had been studying for a while).

1.3 Summary

Introduction provided an overview of the current research and trends in research for Chinese international students. Chinese college ELs face numerous barriers to academic success. Reading comprehension, a process to extract and construct meaning by interacting with written language, is the most important component of academic literacy. International college students perform more poorly on tests of reading comprehension than their English-speaking peers. However, little research has explored Chinese international college students' English reading comprehension development. Likewise, ELs' self-perception of English ability matters to their English achievement. Self-perception of English ability is vigorously shaped by people's experiences. Thus, it is important to understand students' perception of their experiences. The results may highlight the importance of increasing the awareness of cultural diversity in U.S. higher education and better supporting international students to be successful in international higher education.

Chapter 2 Theoretical Framework and Literature Review

In this chapter, the theories and research related to my study were provided. The first section described the theoretical framework that offered a foundation for my work. The second section depicted the literature review that specifically introduced the current and past research in the field.

2.1 Theoretical Framework

Some relevant theories were explored, including social constructivism theory, sociocultural second language acquisition (SLA), schema theory, and transformative learning theory. This section also talked about academic literacy, disciplinary literacy, and reading comprehension. Thus, I could better understand how immersion in an authentic English-speaking environment contributed to individuals' overall learning, language acquisition and learning, and reading comprehension.

2.1.1 Social Constructivism Theory

Social constructivism theory (Vygotsky, 1978, 1986) describes how learners construct their knowledge through social interactions. Children's learning, including but not limited to knowledge, ideas, attitudes, and values, mostly comes from the people around them with whom they interact. For example, Vygotsky argued that children's language mastery most influenced their learning because children used their language as a tool to think about and respond to the world (Tracey & Morrow, 2012). Vygotsky's concept of the Zone of Proximal Development (ZPD) is also influential. The ZPD refers to the ideal level of task difficulty to facilitate students' learning at which a student can succeed with appropriate support (Temple et al., 2011). Tasks that students can complete independently do not fall in the ZPD. Therefore, these tasks are not ideal to improve students' learning (Tracey & Morrow, 2012). For example, for the tasks that students can finish independently, they are not in the ZPD and would not likely promote the students' learning. Vygotsky's theories of learning are relevant to my study because he has emphasized the important role of language and dialogue in learning and has suggested tasks with appropriate support can ideally facilitate learners' learning. For example, for my study, when Chinese students are exposed to the ESL context, they meet various language tasks with difficulty and some tasks in the ZPD will perfectly facilitate students' learning. Meanwhile, students' English language improvement in an authentic English-speaking environment will promote their English reading comprehension.

2.1.2 Sociocultural Second Language Acquisition

Ellis (2015) stated that L2 learning was a process rather than a product because all L2 learning was local and took place in a particular situation. Language is tied to context and can only be modified or extended in the same or new context. Therefore, L2 learning is seen as an ongoing process that is connected to the context of language use. For instance, English learners in the ESL context experience the use of routines and linguistic forms in continuing and authentic English-speaking situations. This is important to my work because Chinese students' English reading comprehension will continue to develop when they are exposed to an authentic English-speaking environment.

2.1.3 Schema Theory

Schema theory is one constructivist theory. It indicates "people have schemata for everything in their lives including people, places, things, language, processes, and skills" (Tracey & Morrow, 2012, p. 62), and everyone has an individual schema (Cobb & Kallus, 2011). For instance, a horse rider has a much different schema for horses than someone who has never ridden a horse.

Anderson and Pearson (1984) asserted readers had their schemas for content, reading processes, and different text structures. For instance, a reader has a schema for people, places, and things in the text. During the reading process, she/he has a schema for decoding, skimming, inferencing, or summarizing. Also, a reader has a schema for narrative and expository texts. Therefore, differences in readers' schemas result in differences in reading comprehension. For example, a person who has a detailed schema for fishing would comprehend a text related to that topic differently compared with a reader who has limited experience with or knowledge of fishing. Besides, developing readers' schemas in the areas of skills and text structures will influence their reading comprehension (Tracey & Morrow, 2012). For example, a reader who has many schemas for reading skills and different text structures will more easily comprehend the texts than someone who has limited knowledge of skills and text structures.

Students who have grown up in China and students who have grown up
in the U.S. are likely to have very different schemas including social practices,
values, beliefs, languages, worldviews, and scientific themes. Some research
shows that the differences between East Asian and Western students in reading
comprehension depend on the different philosophies people believe in (Nisbett,
2003). For example, Nisbett (2003) showed that many Chinese put confidence
in Confucianism and believed in harmony, self-control, and hierarchy, while a
lot of Americans had faith in Western Enlightenment and accepted
independence, freedom, and equality as true. When dealing with social
conflict, the Chinese develop their dialectic as a cognitive tool because their
social existence is based on harmony. Chinese dialectic is described as a
positive and dialectical logic and emphasizes the relational quality between
good and evil, something and nothing (Chang, 1939). That means the Chinese
might resolve a conflict of views, transcend it, or find a "Middle Way". In
short, they approach issues dialectically. In contrast, Americans are free to
argue and develop rules for debate, "including the principle of noncontradiction
and formal logic" (Nisbett, 2003, p. 37). So, Chinese students are used to
applying their dialectic to questions, whereas American students employ logic
for problems. These irreconcilable differences can result in the differences in
reading comprehension between Chinese and American students. Thus, different
contexts can eventually influence readers' comprehension.

2.1.4 Transformative Learning Theory

Another major guiding theory of this study is Mezirow's (1991) transformative
learning theory. Mezirow (1991) developed transformative learning theory:

that can explain how adult learners make sense or meaning of their experiences, the nature of the structures that influence the way they construe experience, the dynamics involved in modifying meanings, and the structures of meaning themselves undergo changes when learners find them to be dysfunctional (p. xii).

Mezirow (1991) introduced the 10 stages of transformative learning:

(1) A disorienting dilemma, (2) Self-examination with feelings of guilt or shame, (3) A critical assessment of epistemic, sociocultural, or psychic assumptions, (4) Recognition that one's discontent and the process of transformation are shared and that others have negotiated a similar change, (5) Exploration of options for new roles, relationships, and actions, (6) Planning a course of action, (7) Acquisition of knowledge and skills for implementing one's plans, (8) Provisional trying of new roles, (9) Building of competence and self-confidence in new roles and relationships; and (10) A reintegration into one's life on the basis of conditions dictated by one's new perspective. (p. 168-169)

Chinese students might experience some stages of transformative learning when they transferred from the EFL context to the ESL environment. The authentic English-speaking environment would greatly influence their perception of academic reading comprehension. Thus, their perception would be changed over time.

2.1.5 Academic Literacy and Disciplinary Literacy

Academic literacy and disciplinary literacy play critical roles in student college success. Academic literacy is referred to as proficiency in reading and writing about academic subjects (Neeley, 2005). It is also a generic ability to be developed in academic contexts for students and plays an important role in students' academic success. Weideman (2007, 2018) demonstrated 10 components of academic literacy, including (1) understanding academic vocabulary, (2) metaphor and idiom, (3) understanding relations between different parts of a text, (4) understanding text genre, (5) interpreting graphic and visual information, (6) distinguishing between essential and non-essential information, (7) sequencing, ordering, and simple numerical computation, (8) finding evidence, making inferences, and extrapolating, (9) understanding communicative function, and (10) making meaning beyond the sentence. Short and Fitzsimmons (2007) expanded the definition of academic literacy. They stated that academic literacy not only involved reading, writing, discourse for school, knowledge of multiple genres of text, purposes of text use, and text media, but also was affected by students' literacies in contexts outside of school, and student's personal, social, and cultural experiences.

Disciplinary literacy is referred to as discipline-specific literacy, in which different content experts employ discipline-specific practices such as reading, speaking, writing, viewing, visually representing, and reasoning to learn and communicate (Conley, 2008; Moje, 2008; Shanahan et al., 2011). Disciplinary literacy is different from general academic literacy as disciplinary literacy aims to develop students' ability to use "specialized literacy skills, strategies, and practices to engage in disciplinary learning and socialization", in short, it is described as "disciplinary habits of mind" (Fang & Coatoam, 2013, p. 628). For example, the field of statistics has a very different discipline-specific literacy from the field of history.

2.1.6 Reading Comprehension

Reading comprehension is defined as a process to extract and construct meaning by interacting with written language. Readers have to employ a wide range of knowledge, skills, and strategies to construct meaning (Snow, 2002). For example, readers make sense of a text from the information on the page and thoughts and ideas evoked by the text (Schoenbach et al., 2012). Reading comprehension is a challenge for L2 learners because it is a complex interaction of text, reader, and contextual factors (Duke et al., 2011; Duke & Carlisle, 2011). It is an ability to construct meaning in a sociocultural context where readers, texts, and contexts transact (Almasi & Fullerton, 2012). The main theory of reading comprehension is constructivism.

2.2 Literature Review

The beginning of this part presented an overview of Chinese international students in the U.S., general and language-specific factors influencing Chinese students, and students' perception of English ability. The next part talked about college students' reading comprehension in academic literacy and disciplinary literacy and L2 learners' reading comprehension in college academic contexts. The rest of the articles introduced the assessments of reading comprehension in general and in ELs.

2.2.1 An Overview of Chinese International Students in the U. S.

According to the *Open Doors Report on International Educational Exchange* (IIE, 2019), U. S. universities continue to attract large numbers of international students including undergraduate and graduate students. In 2019, 1,095,299 international students attended higher education in the U.S., which made up 5.5 percent of the total U. S. higher education population. China remained the largest source of international students in 2018/19 with 369,548 students enrolled in undergraduate, graduate, non-degree, and optional practical training programs, accounting for roughly 30% of all foreign students (IIE, 2019).

International students are referred to as "second language students born, raised, and educated in another country who come temporarily to the U.S. on a foreign student visa for a short-term educational or training program" (Ferris, 2009, p. 4). Many international students tend to go back to their home countries once they complete their programs (Zhang-Wu, 2018). International students usually face cultural and language barriers that impede their academic achievement (Smith, 2007).

2.2.2 General Factors Influencing Chinese Students

Research shows that Chinese international students face some challenges in U. S. universities, including the English language, American classroom structure, and emotional issues (Liu, 2016). These issues are important to my study because they all affect students' reading comprehension. For example, Chinese students lack listening, speaking, and writing skills (Abelmann & Kang, 2014; Tweed & Lehman, 2002; Yeh & Inose, 2003; Liu, 2016).

Listening, speaking, and writing are basic language skills for ELs and they are also linguistic factors that influence ELs' reading comprehension (Kern, 1988). Chinese students also encounter different classroom structures because Chinese professors focus more on lectures, notes written on the blackboard, lecture summaries, and the use of textbooks (Bartlett & Fischer, 2011; Tweed & Lehman, 2002; Wang, 2013; Jinyan, 2005). These classroom structures could affect students' cognitive processes and eventually influence their reading comprehension (August et al., 2006). Additionally, Chinese international students face loneliness and stress (Fischer, 2012; McClure, 2007; Liu, 2016). As we know, loneliness and stress put up affective barriers, which can affect readers' comprehension (Kern, 1988).

Ching et al. (2017) offered a comprehensive description of the challenges that influenced Chinese international students' study and life in U.S. universities. These included the following: (1) cultural distance, (2) cultural shock, (3) social support, (4) stress and anxiety, (5) language barriers, and (6) classroom transition (Ching et al., 2017). Among these barriers, language issues directly affect students' reading comprehension, whereas others affect the affective aspects of learning and learners' comprehension and learning.

Huang (2012) described Chinese international students experienced frustrations transitioning to American university classrooms because of the cultural and educational differences between China and the U.S. For example, classroom structures in an American university, such as class discussions, required group work, and lack of notes written on the board, are very different from the Chinese classroom. Class discussion is not familiar to Chinese students as it is not polite to constantly talk about personal opinions in the Chinese culture (Ching et al., 2017). Also, discussion with professors is not appropriate because professors are viewed as authority figures in their fields and Chinese students may not feel comfortable challenging their professors' opinions (Huang, 2012). These distinctions may become cognitive barriers and affect students' comprehension and learning. Furthermore, Huang (2012) stated that Chinese students were not familiar with learning materials, especially for the social sciences which were more likely relevant to American culture, so they may have to spend more time and make more efforts to synthesize information to resolve these cognitive conflicts than their American peers. This also influences Chinese students' reading comprehension because background knowledge plays an important role in readers' comprehension and readers who are more familiar with the topic may better understand the text (Artelt et al., 2001; August et al., 2006).

Normally, Chinese students do well in American higher education with personal efforts and high motivation (Kaufman, 2004; Zhou et al., 2003). However, research shows they have emotional issues like loneliness and stress (Fischer, 2012; McClure, 2007). Chinese international students also lack a familiar cultural and linguistic environment, and they miss their families and friends (Fischer, 2012; McClure, 2007; Sawir et al., 2008; Zhao et al., 2008; Ip et al., 2009). Also, they have fewer connections with American peers (Fischer, 2012; Gareis, 2012). They need social support and connectedness to help them succeed in a new environment (Sherry et al., 2010; Suido et al., 2008). These emotional issues make up affective factors that may influence Chinese students' reading comprehension. Also, these issues place great demands on students' cognitive loads. Cooper (1998) defined a cognitive load as the "total amount of mental energy imposed on working memory at an instance in time" (p. 10). The cognitive load also contributes to L2 reading comprehension. In other words, if there are more cognitive demands, there is less mental energy for comprehension (Bailey & Pransky, 2014).

2.2.3 Language-specific Factors Influencing Chinese Students

Empirical evidence shows that English language proficiency plays an important role in international students' academic and social success (Andrade, 2006; Yeh & Inose, 2003; Sawir, 2005). In general, Chinese students have learned English for years in China before they study abroad. Although they generally have high performance on TOEFL and IELTS exams, Chinese international students are severely under-prepared for an authentic English-speaking environment (Wang, 2016). Wang (2003) recognized some key challenges for Chinese international students, including the impact of Chinese language expressions, lacking contextual knowledge or background knowledge, and being short of English practice and training (e.g. reading, writing, and oral English skills). These key challenges can affect comprehension. For example, knowledge of idiomatic expressions and contextual/background knowledge are key elements that contribute to comprehension. Also, oral English proficiency is needed to help students understand lectures or in-class discussions. Thus, Chinese students' English deficiency deeply affects their comprehension in an authentic English-speaking environment.

Fu et al. (2018) used mixed methods to explore factors influencing Chinese international students' strategic language learning at ten universities in the U.S. Data were collected in two phases including 15 interviewees from four U.S. universities and 117 responses from six U.S. universities. All participants were Chinese international students above the age of 18 in the undergraduate and graduate programs in the U.S. and had lived in the U.S. for less than 10 years. The authors identified 9 factors predicting respondents' use of language learning strategies such as: "(1) learning preferences; (2) motivation of English learning; (3) skills and learning content required by majors; (4) active class participation promoted by instructors; (5) critical thinking skills promoted by instructors; (6) variety of assessments used by instructors; (7) instructor availability in and after class; (8) immersion in an authentic English-speaking environment, and (9) exposure to the social and cultural values of the U.S." (Fu et al., 2018, p. 1898). Some of the factors are most relevant to my study because they can influence students' reading comprehension. For example, Hidi (2001) claimed that individual interest had a strong positive influence on readers' comprehension and learning. Likewise, skills and learning content required by majors and critical thinking skills could help students comprehend in disciplinary learning (Fang & Coatoam, 2013).

In summary, Chinese international students face some obstacles in American higher education, and some challenges can affect students' reading comprehension, including their English language proficiency, different classroom structures, and their emotional issues. But we still do not know whether and how immersion in an authentic English-speaking environment and exposure to the social and cultural values of the U.S. could influence Chinese students' reading comprehension. Longcope (2009) developed one study to examine six Japanese adult students who participated in a summer study abroad program to compare the EFL and ESL learning contexts. The participants filled out questionnaires regarding their English usage before and during the study abroad program. The results found according to an interaction-by-interaction basis, learners in the ESL context obtained more comprehensible input and thus "produce more comprehensible output and negotiate for meaning more with their interlocutors" (Longcope, 2009, p. 317) than those in the EFL context. However, this research focused on oral language, and little research examined how immersion in an authentic English-speaking environment contributed to Chinese students' reading comprehension. My study is trying to fill some of these gaps by exploring Chinese students' reading comprehension development in an authentic English-speaking environment.

2.2.4 Students' Self-perception of English Ability

Students' self-perception of English ability is considerably related to their academic achievement (Usher & Pajares, 2008). Research has firmly established that native English speakers who have high reading self-efficacy beliefs perform better on reading comprehension tests (Barkley, 2006; Liew et al., 2008; Mucherah & Yoder, 2008). Even low achievers with positive self-efficacy beliefs present better in reading than low achievers with negative self-efficacy beliefs (Shell et al., 1995).

English learners' self-perception of English ability is one of the essential factors which may influence English learning and acquisition (Onwuegbuzie et al., 1999). Takahashi (2009) investigated 98 Japanese college students and found out that there was a positive correlation between students' self-perception of English ability and their English achievement. In other words, students who perceived themselves as having higher English ability demonstrated higher English proficiency. Hall (2012) stated that self-perception of English ability was powerfully shaped by people's experiences. So, it is necessary to understand students' experiences. My study is not just about understanding students' perception and experiences, but also about exploring how their perception might align with their actual English ability and development.

2.2.5 College Students' Reading Comprehension

Hock et al. (2015) defined "reading comprehension as a process in which the reader constructs meaning from text-based information and information the reader has previously acquired through formal learning or life experiences" (p. 177). It involves readers, texts, and activity so that it is also an ability to understand a text and integrate it with readers' background knowledge (Grabe, 2009; RAND Reading Study Group & Snow, 2002). Reading comprehension is a critical skill for college students in both general academic literacy and discipline-specific literacy.

2.2.5.1 College Students' Reading Comprehension in Academic Literacy

Normally, the components of academic literacy are measured by text comprehension (Weideman, 2018). Thus, reading comprehension plays an important role in academic literacy, and it is also a critical skill for college academic success. Over the past decades, many studies have emphasized specific factors (e.g. vocabulary knowledge), which are best to predict reading comprehension in general academic literacy. For example, August et al. (2006) combined language skills and cognitive processes and indicated that reading comprehension depended on decoding skills, knowledge in some domains (e.g. vocabulary, linguistic structure, and discourses), and cognitive processing capacities (e.g. text memory, background knowledge, justified inferences).

Some scholars have expanded on the factors that affect college students' reading comprehension. For example, Taub and Benson (2013) employed the Cattell-Horn-Carroll (CHC) theoretical model to examine the effects of seven broad factors on college students' reading comprehension. The seven broad factors include auditory processing, crystallized intelligence, fluid reasoning, long-term retrieval, processing speed, short-term memory, and visual-spatial thinking. The sample included 1,423 college students with ages ranging from 20 to 39. The sample included traditional students who had completed at least one year of college and nontraditional students through the age of 39. However, we do not know whether these students are native English speakers or L2 learners. Thus, we are not sure if the CHC model applies to L2 speakers. The results indicated only crystallized intelligence (e. g. word knowledge, verbal intelligence, syntactical knowledge, and semantic processing), and visual-spatial thinking (e. g. alphabetic coding, letter-identification, and visual discrimination) had statistically significant direct effects on the successful reading comprehension of college students. This study represented the first time visual-spatial thinking demonstrated statistically significant direct effects on reading comprehension. It is important to mention that Chinese students have different approaches to visual-spatial thinking because Chinese college students prefer visual learning which means a learner uses graphs, charts, maps, and diagrams to learn (Sun, 2011). Sun connected these preferences to the Chinese traditional way of teaching and the pictorial nature of Chinese characters. Specifically, Chinese teachers from elementary school to college always offer presentations and write much important information on the blackboard, and students must write down everything they have heard and seen in the classroom. Additionally, Chinese characters are ideograms, and each character looks like a picture. However, we are not sure if and how visual-spatial thinking contributes to Chinese students' L2 reading comprehension. Thus, it is necessary to do a study with Chinese international students to understand their reading comprehension development of academic literacy.

2.2.5.2 College Students' Reading Comprehension in Disciplinary Literacy

More recently, people have begun to realize that disciplinary or content area reading comprehension plays a crucial role in college academic success. For example, Fang and Pace (2013) found that readers were required to have specific language knowledge, disciplinary knowledge, and close reading when reading disciplinary texts. Close reading normally involves profound questions, rereading, and discussion of high-quality texts. Usually, successful students can employ general literacy skills and strategies, prior knowledge of content, and disciplinary-specific skills and strategies to understand texts (Wang, 2019). However, the main emphasis in research still "has been on general reading comprehension or study skills strategies within the context of subject matter materials" (Herber, 1970; McKenna & Robinson, 1990; Moje et al., 2000; O'Brien et al., 1995; Rycik & Irvin, 2001; Vacca, 2002 as cited in Shanahan et al., 2011, p. 394).

Some scholars have examined the factors that influence students' reading comprehension in discipline-specific literacy. For instance, Ozuru et al. (2009) investigated how text cohesion, reading skills, and prior knowledge contributed to college aged students' biology text comprehension. Text cohesion refers to how the text helps the readers establish a coherent understanding of the text. For example, many textbooks use section headings as a way to organize content coherently. There were two groups of participants involved in this study. One group had 108 undergraduate students enrolled in an introductory psychology course at the University of Memphis. The other group included 62 undergraduate students enrolled in an introductory biology course at Old Dominion University. The two universities were comparable based on the college ranking report in the *U.S. News* in 2007. The two groups of students were similar in reading skills. Students' text comprehension was measured with open-ended comprehension questions that assessed different levels of comprehension (i.e. text-based, local-bridging, and global-bridging). Results demonstrated that (1) high text cohesion improved students' text-based comprehension, (2) students' overall reading comprehension was positively correlated with their prior knowledge, and (3) students with more reading skills benefited more from high-cohesion texts. This study is important to my study because it could be concluded that text cohesion, reading skills, and prior knowledge all influence college students' reading comprehension in disciplinary literacy. However, we do not know whether these college students are native speakers or L2 learners.

Moreover, Kendeou et al. (2011) investigated the effects of readers' epistemic beliefs and text structure on the comprehension processes of reading scientific texts. Epistemic beliefs refer to individuals' beliefs about the nature of knowledge and knowing (Hofer & Pintrich, 1997; Schommer, 1990). Schommer (1990) classified five beliefs, including (1) simple knowledge (i.e. knowledge consists of discrete facts), (2) certain knowledge (i. e. absolute knowledge exists and will eventually be known), (3) omniscient authority (i.e. authorities have access to otherwise inaccessible knowledge), (4) quick learning (i. e. learning occurs in a quick or not-at-all fashion), and (5) innate ability (i. e. the ability to acquire knowledge is endowed at birth). Later, Schommer (1994) identified there was a relation between epistemic beliefs and reading comprehension. Generally, people with more sophisticated epistemic beliefs think that knowledge is complex, tentative, and evolving, while people with less sophisticated epistemic beliefs consider that knowledge is simple, absolute, and certain (Murphy & Mason, 2006). The sample included 28 female and 18 male undergraduates at McGill University in Canada. The results indicated students with more sophisticated epistemic beliefs engaged in more conceptual change processes than students with less sophisticated epistemic beliefs when reading a refutation text. The refutation text structure is one kind of expository text structure and aims to persuade people to change their prior beliefs by identifying misconceptions and explaining the correct ideas. Conceptual change processes are referred to as responses that can indicate readers are engaging in conceptual change, such as experiencing cognitive conflict, responding to conflict, and contrasting information. This study is relevant to my study as individuals' epistemic beliefs strongly influence expository text comprehension in disciplinary literacy. Also, there are cultural differences in epistemic beliefs. For example, Ren (2006) found the significant differences between American and Chinese college students in the epistemic beliefs of simple knowledge, certain knowledge, omniscient authority, and quick learning. Hardy and Tolhurst (2014) claimed that "Through diligence and effort in repeatedly reading the material from different perspectives, students from non-Western backgrounds can develop a deep understanding of learning material, while in the process committing to memory important detail" (p. 275).

2.2.5.3 L2 Learners' Reading Comprehension in College Academic Contexts

Reading comprehension is a fundamental skill not only for native speakers but also for L2 learners in college academic contexts. Learning academic literacy is a big challenge for ELs. Curry (2004) represented that ELs had difficulties in college academic literacy, including engaging in a variety of academic social practices and negotiating multiple academic discourses in various circumstances. Lei et al. (2010) also indicated that even at the college level ELs faced many obstacles in academic literacy. For example, many college ELs lack academic vocabulary, and they are not familiar with English metaphors and idioms, and different text genres.

Additionally, L2 reading comprehension is more complicated because it also depends on learners' L1 reading ability and L2 proficiency. For example, Bernhardt (2005) demonstrated that L2 language proficiency accounted for around 30% of the variance in L2 reading comprehension, whereas L1 reading ability accounted for 14%–21%. But she lacked data from non-syllabic languages. Moreover, the study identified that L1–L2 orthographic distance could impact learning to read in the context of L2 (Wang & Koda, 2005; Koda, 2007). Learners with alphabetic L1 orthographic backgrounds (e. g. Spanish, Indonesian, and Korean) have more advantages in L2 reading in English than those with non-alphabetic L1 backgrounds (e.g. Chinese and Japanese) because of the intra-word analysis experience in processing alphabets in L1.

After measuring 246 Chinese college students learning English, Jiang (2011) revealed that L1 reading ability as an important predictor of L2 reading may not apply as well with Chinese ELs due to the large L1–L2 orthographic distance. Chinese has a logographic orthographic system, and the writing system is based on characters that are tied to meaning instead of sound. That is very different from English which uses a sound-based orthographic system.

Besides ELs' first language and English proficiency, some studies have emphasized using a variety of strategies to improve ELs' reading comprehension and academic achievement. For instance, Zhang (1992) examined the effects of teaching reading strategies on improving reading comprehension for adult ELs. There were 29 students at the University of Alabama in an academic English program involved in this study. The sample included 46.7% Japanese, 16.7% Korean, 10% Saudi Arabian, 6.7% Chinese, 6.7% Brazilian, 6.7% Venezuelan,

3.3% Costa Rican, and 3.3% Thai students. The results showed that the introduction of reading strategies, particularly memory, cognitive, and compensation strategies, did help students make improvements in reading comprehension, supporting previous research findings (Scarella & Oxford, 1992). By contrast, Mihara (2011) argued that some reading strategies (e. g. vocabulary pre-teaching, comprehension question presentation) had fewer effects on Japanese adult ELs' reading comprehension. But we are not sure if and how these reading strategies affect Chinese adult ELs' reading comprehension, and thus there will be more research encouraged.

Perez and Holmes (2010) provided cognitive, metacognitive, and social/ affective learning strategies for ELs to ensure academic literacy. The authors suggested that EL students "use their existing knowledge and conceptual development from their native language to support the acquisition of academic literacy skills in English" (p. 36). ELs must have explicit instruction on reading comprehension strategies as ELs may not transfer the strategies to English even if they know how to apply such strategies in their native languages.

Overall, after exploring college students' reading comprehension in academic literacy and disciplinary literacy, and ELs' reading comprehension in college academic contexts, it is rare to find research that has emphasized Chinese students' academic reading comprehension. Therefore, my study is attempting to fill the gap to understand Chinese international students' reading comprehension development of academic literacy.

2.2.6 Assessments of Reading Comprehension

Generally, reading comprehension is measured by a series of questions or by a cloze task after reading a passage (Nag, 2017b; Zuilkowski et al., 2019). Comprehension questions have two general types, including literal and inferential questions. Literal questions ask readers to find specific details in the text, whereas inferential questions require readers to combine information from the text and make an inference (Miller & Smith, 1984). A cloze test (maze or open-ended) asks readers to complete an argument or a predicate with three-word choices in the maze format or with a blank in the open-ended format (Williams et al., 2011). Cloze tests have been widely used for K-12 grades (Shin et al., 2000; Wiley & Deno, 2005; Brown-Chidsey et al., 2003) and adult ELs (Kobayashi, 2002; Yamashita, 2003).

Additionally, Informal Reading Inventories (IRIs) are the individual administrated diagnostic assessments constructed to evaluate a student's strengths and weaknesses in reading performance (Nilsson, 2008). Typically, IRIs include graded word lists and passages (Paris & Carpenter, 2003). A student reads each leveled passage and answers the questions orally to measure his/her comprehension and recall (Nilsson, 2008). IRIs are informal assessments that are commonly utilized by teachers to measure students' ongoing literacy development. Generally, teachers and reading specialists use IRIs to assess K-12 students' reading performance. IRIs can be beneficial instruments for ELs as ELs' literacy development does not always match their grade level placement due to their diverse backgrounds (Cloud et al., 2009). However, little research examines if and how IRIs can be used to measure college ELs' reading comprehension.

2.2.6.1 Reading Comprehension Assessments for College Students

Sustained silent reading tests have been widely used in some large-scale measure tools to assess individuals' reading comprehension performance, including the National Assessment of Educational Progress (National Center for Educational Statistics, 2001), the Programme for International Student Assessment (Organisation for Economic Cooperation and Development, 2001), the Progress in International Reading Literacy Study (International Association for the Evaluation of Educational Achievement, 2001) for children and adolescents, and the National Assessment of Adult Literacy (National Center for Education Statistics, 2003) and International Adult Literacy Survey for adults (Williams et al., 2011). The sustained silent reading test asks readers to read extended passages and then answer a series of multiple-choice comprehension questions (e.g. literal and inferential questions).

Some researchers indicated that sustained silent reading tests may not be best suited to measure college students' reading comprehension because some comprehension questions can be answered correctly regardless of the passages. For example, Keenan and Betjemann (2006) examined the validity of the sustained silent reading test of the Gray Oral Reading Test (GORT; Wiederholt & Bryant, 1992, 2001). The results showed that native English-speaking undergraduates were able to answer 86% of comprehension questions correctly without reading the passages. Similarly, Coleman et al. (2008) argued against the validity of the sustained silent reading test of the Nelson-Denny Reading Comprehension (NDRC; Brown et al., 1993). The NDRC is a standardized assessment that involves seven passages with 38 comprehension questions (i.e. 19 literal and 19 inferential questions). Passages include a variety of domains of knowledge. Coleman et al. (2008) reported that native English-speaking undergraduates were able to answer 46% of the questions on Form G and 49% of the questions on Form H of the NDRC without reading the passages. In contrast, Williams et al. (2011) confirmed that the sustained silent reading test of the NDRC had good concurrent validity with two types of cloze tests (i.e. maze and open-ended) after examining 100 college native speakers by Form H of the NDRC. So, it seems that there is some disagreement in the field about the validity of these assessments. Additionally, as all participants are native English-speaking college students, we are not sure if and how sustained silent reading tests are best suited to assess college L2 learners' reading comprehension.

Some researchers have employed cloze tests to measure college students' reading comprehension ability. For example, Everatt (1997) reported that struggling college native speakers had difficulty with open-ended cloze tests due to their low verbal ability. The students had average or above intelligence but had a formal dyslexia diagnosis.

Williams et al. (2011) compared the maze and open-ended cloze tests among adult native speakers. The results showed that the maze cloze test did well in discriminating between struggling and non-struggling college readers, and it offered an assessment of global comprehension (i.e. fluency, decoding, inferential comprehension) for adult learners. In contrast, the open-ended cloze test is limited to the measurement of reading comprehension in the adult population. However, all subjects in these studies were native English-speaking adults. We still do not know whether and how cloze tests (maze or open-ended) work for adult/college ELs.

2.2.6.2 Reading Comprehension Assessments for International Students

Usually, international students' reading comprehension is assessed prior to admission when they take the TOEFL or IELTS assessment, the two major assessments for identifying international college ELs' English proficiency for academic admission for colleges and universities in the U.S., Canada, and other parts of the world (ETS, 2010).

The TOEFL iBT is more common and comprises four sections: listening, reading, speaking, and writing. Its reading section has two formats. The short format includes three passages, while the long format involves five passages. Each passage has approximately 700 words. Readers need to answer 12−14 questions after each passage. Most questions are multiple-choice questions. Test takers are given 60 minutes to read all the passages and respond to the questions for the short format, and 100 minutes for the long format. Only three passages of the long format will be used for scoring purposes, and the other two passages will be evaluated by ETS for future use.

Likewise, the IELTS comes in two types: academic and general training. The academic type is widely used for people entering university or seeking professional registration. Each type consists of four sections: reading, writing, listening, and speaking. The IELTS academic reading section involves three long texts and 40 questions. Question types vary, including multiple-choice, identifying information, identifying the writer's views/claims, matching information, matching headings, matching features, matching sentence endings, sentence completion, summarizing, table, flow-chart completion, diagram label completion, and short-answer questions. Readers have 60 minutes to complete all passages and questions.

ETS (2010) conducted a research study to compare scores between the TOEFL and the IELTS. The sample was 1,153 students who had taken both tests. The largest group was from China, accounting for 41% of all participants. ETS compared two scores of each section (i.e. listening, speaking, reading, and writing) and the total test. The results indicated that most of the takers scored in the middle to mid-high score ranges on both tests. For example, TOEFL reading scores of 19 to 23 may correspond to an IELTS reading score of 6.5. TOEFL reading scores of 24 to 26 may correspond to an IELTS reading score of 7.0, and so forth. The TOEFL and the IELTS examine students' general reading abilities, but they are not necessarily reading comprehension assessments.

2.3 Summary

This chapter introduced the major theoretical bases for this study, including social constructivism theory, sociocultural second language acquisition, schema theory, and transformative learning theory. This section also talked about academic literacy, disciplinary literacy, and reading comprehension. These helped me better understand how immersion in an authentic English-speaking environment contributed to individuals' overall learning, language acquisition and learning, and reading comprehension. In addition, this chapter contained a review of literature on the past and current research regarding Chinese international students, which focused on an overview of Chinese international students in the U.S., general and language-specific factors influencing Chinese students, students' perception of English ability, college students' reading comprehension in academic literacy and disciplinary literacy, L2 learners' reading comprehension in college academic context, and the assessments of reading comprehension in general and in ELs.

Chapter 3 Methodology

This chapter introduced the methods I used in conducting my work, including research questions, research design, population and sample, confidentiality, access, and informed consent, data sources and data collection, data analysis, and researcher positionality.

3.1 Research Questions

The purpose of this study was to describe and understand Chinese international students' perception of how exposure to the authentic English-speaking environment contributed to their reading comprehension development of academic literacy.

The following questions guided the study:

RQ1: What perception did Chinese international students have about their English reading comprehension in academic literacy when they were first exposed to the authentic English-speaking environment?

RQ2: How does Chinese international students' initial perception change after years of exposure to the authentic English-speaking environment?

RQ3: How does Chinese international students' self-perception of their English reading comprehension relate to their actual reading comprehension performance?

RQ4: How do Chinese international students perceive the English-speaking environment contributes to their development of academic reading comprehension?

3.2 Research Design

This study used a qualitative research method (Denzin & Lincoln, 2005) and a descriptive case study design (Merriam, 1998). A qualitative research method seeks to investigate a phenomenon by exploring individuals' perspectives and the phenomenon's real-world context (Denzin & Lincoln, 2005). Also, qualitative research aims to help researchers to gain a deeper understanding of the phenomena (Tracy, 2013). Thus, the qualitative research method was appropriate for my work because the purpose of this study was to gain a deeper understanding of how exposure to the authentic English- speaking environment contributed to Chinese students' reading comprehension development, through describing and understanding their thoughts, perception, and experiences regarding reading comprehension development when they studied in an American university.

This study utilized a multiple descriptive case study design. A case study can be used to investigate events, situations, and activities by describing one or more cases (Merriam, 1998). It emphasizes examining a phenomenon within the real-world context (Yin, 2014). My participants in this study took a comprehension assessment to measure their current background knowledge, reading rate, and reading comprehension. A week later, they responded to a series of interview questions regarding their reading comprehension development by reflecting on their experiences of exposure to the authentic English-speaking environment.

A descriptive case study can provide a detailed account of the study under investigation (Merriam, 1998). It requires an accurate description of a phenomenon in its real-world context (Yin, 2014). The researcher seeks to identify characteristics, behaviors, and patterns (Tracy, 2013). The descriptive case study applied to my work because the participants of this study were Chinese international students, who were a specific population at an American university in the mid-South. Additionally, I had the intent of describing and understanding the perception of Chinese international students regarding their reading comprehension development.

3.3 Population and Sample

The population of this study included all Chinese international students from China at a university in the mid-South, including undergraduate and graduate students. Based on this university's international center (2020)'s report, there were 462 Chinese international undergraduate and graduate students enrolled in Spring 2020. I intentionally selected participants who met the required criteria for inclusion. The main criterion for participation was that potential participants had never studied in an English-speaking country before enrolling at the university. Specifically, for undergraduate students, they had never attended American schools or English-medium K-12 schools in China. For graduate students, they must have completed their undergraduate work in China, and they could not have studied in the U.S. or English-medium schools for K-12. These decisions made sure that all participants were newly exposed to the ESL context when they enrolled at the university so that they were sensitive to the English-speaking environment.

This helped me to answer my research question regarding the participants' perception of how reading comprehension developed after exposure to an authentic English-speaking environment. If the participants had already had many years' experiences of exposure to the ESL context, it would be hard to explain how an English-speaking environment influenced students' reading comprehension development. Additionally, I looked for diverse majors because students who were in STEM fields, humanities, or social sciences might have different language demands or language exposure. Therefore, these sampling decisions helped me to make a more rigorous research design.

A purposive sample of Chinese international students was appropriate for my work due to the perception of participants regarding their reading comprehension development. Purposive sampling is utilized to select subjects with specific characteristics from an accessible population (Lewis-Beck et al., 2004). Researchers use a purposive sample to choose participants who represent the available population (Lewis- Beck et al., 2004).

In addition to excluding students who had prior educational experiences in English-speaking countries, I used additional criteria to select participants. The university's international center (2020) reported that out of 462 Chinese degree students enrolled in 2020, 100 were female undergraduate students and 119 were female graduate students, while 115 were male undergraduate students, and 128 were male graduate students. In order to represent the perspectives of different groups of students within Chinese international student population, I recruited four categories of students: female undergraduate, female graduate, male undergraduate, and male graduate. According to Sandelowski (1995), 5 to

20 subjects are an acceptable sample size for a qualitative study (as cited in Nicholson, 2018). Therefore, I recruited 8 Chinese international students to participate in this study, including 2 female undergraduates, 2 female graduates, 2 male undergraduates, and 2 male graduates.

Also, students' different exposure time to the English context was considered so that I could examine if different exposure time contributed to the participants' reading comprehension. I divided students into two groups: students in their first year (to capture early exposure), and students who had been here for more than one year. Thus, in this study, I purposively chose 8 Chinese international students, including (1) one female undergraduate in her first year, (2) one female undergraduate who had been here for more than one year, (3) one female graduate in her first year, (4) one female graduate who had been here for more than one year, (5) one male undergraduate in his first year, (6) one male undergraduate who had been here for more than one year, (7) one male graduate in his first year, and (8) one male graduate who had been here for more than one year.

This study also met the two types of saturation: data saturation and theoretical saturation. Data saturation means continued sampling within a study until the data repeats, while theoretical saturation involves no new themes that have been identified during the process of data analysis (van Rijnsoever, 2017). To ensure data saturation, I kept collecting data until the data repetitions emerged. Likewise, to make sure of theoretical saturation, I analyzed the data until no new themes appeared.

3.4 Confidentiality, Access, and Informed Consent

Confidentiality is essential for all participants. First, I received approval from the University Institutional Review Board (IRB) which offered guidelines and procedures to protect the research participants. Enrollment began upon IRB approval in the fall of 2021. I used WeChat to disseminate the announcement letter to two organizations, the University Chinese Students & Scholars Association (CSSA), and the Graduate and Family Housing Chinese Group, which is a group of WeChat including many Chinese graduate students who live in the Graduate and Family Housing at the university. WeChat is the most popular Chinese multi-purpose messaging, social media, and mobile payment App. WeChat was the only way I distributed the announcement letter. After three distributions of the announcement letter, I received 18 responses from the potential participants via email or WeChat.

When the potential subjects reached me, I conducted a prescreening activity with each of them, including asking about their genders, majors, years in the U.S., and prior experiences with living in an English-speaking country or learning in an English immersion school. After the prescreening, only 11 students met the qualifications. To ensure various majors were included in this descriptive case study, I chose 8 students.

The demographics of the participants are listed below.

Table 3.1　Participant Demographics

Participant	Gender	Age	Major	Education Level	Length of Time in the U.S.
Student A	Female	19	Materials and Engineering Science	Undergraduate	2 months
Student B	Male	20	Electronic Engineering	Undergraduate	2 months
Student C	Female	22	Economics	Undergraduate	2 years
Student D	Male	27	Arts	Undergraduate	3 years
Student E	Female	24	Chemistry	Graduate	3 months
Student F	Male	27	Chemistry	Graduate	3 months
Student G	Female	26	Pharmacology	Graduate	4 years
Student H	Male	29	Education Sciences	Graduate	3 years

Then, each qualified participant was emailed an informed consent form that explained the purpose of this study and the rights of the participants. To establish confidentiality, participants must be respected and be informed about why and how they would be providing information for the study (Castillo-Montoya, 2016). The participants understood that they were asked to provide their verbal consent. During the Zoom meeting, I went through the informed consent form with the participants before doing the assessment activity, asked if they had any questions, and then secured their verbal consent.

The consent was addressed in English in which the participants were proficient. Although the participants are non-native speakers of English, they all passed the TOEFL or the IELTS and met the English language proficiency requirements for admission to U.S. institutions of higher education. They were competent enough to complete a consent process in English. So, evaluating the level of English comprehension was not necessary for my participants.

The participants' privacy was protected in several ways. I protected the participants' privacy through pseudonyms. Recordings and transcripts were saved on password-protected devices. Demographic records with real names were saved on an encrypted USB recording device and were stored in a secure container. Additionally, the participants were able to choose their own pseudonyms to protect their identities. It was suitable to give them a choice because it helped to provide more autonomy and control for them. I did not keep the information I collected from people who did not wind up being participants in the study.

3.5 Data Sources and Data Collection

The purpose of this study was to allow Chinese international students to describe their perception and experiences on academic reading comprehension development after different levels of exposure to the English-speaking environment. Gubrium and Holstein (2003) stated that interviews, observations, and document analysis were major ways for qualitative researchers to generate and gather data. The primary data sources of this descriptive case study involved audiotaped interviews, audiotaped comprehension assessments, and documents representing learners' English ability.

3.5.1 Interviews

Focused interviews were conducted in this study. Yin (2009) claimed that focused interviews were more likely to be used when participants had a short time for interviewing (i. e. an hour). The purpose of focused interview questions is to confirm events that may have already taken place (Yin, 2009). It is also to probe participants for their perspectives. So, researchers must carefully put forward the interview questions to ensure that participants can provide new and authentic answers. Probing questions are necessary to prevent participants from repeating the same information.

I developed open-ended interview questions that aligned with research questions. Castillo-Montoya (2016) asserted that this alignment could eliminate needless questions to increase the effectiveness of the interview questions. Research questions are different from the interview questions. Research questions aim to articulate what the researcher understands whereas the interview questions are to obtain what participants understand (Castillo-Montoya, 2016). For this study, I used interview questions to describe and understand the perception of Chinese international students regarding their academic reading comprehension development. Also, I was aiming to understand their experiences after immersion in the authentic English environment. I aligned the interview questions with the research questions and also formulated these interview questions to better understand the phenomenon that was under the investigation. For example, below are two of the interview questions (see Appendix 1) aligned with research questions:

• What has helped you to feel more comfortable with English?

• What kinds of things do you do to support yourself to continue learning English?

I completed two rounds of interviews for each participant. During the first round of the interviews, subjects took the reading comprehension assessment in English (described later). They read aloud the passage and answered the questions. It took approximately an hour to complete the assessment. During the second round of the interviews, I conducted the interviews in Chinese, our native language, to obtain rich and deep responses. The interview questions were related to their English learning experiences. It took about one hour to complete each interview. Interviews were transcribed from Chinese recordings to English-written transcripts by myself. All assessments and interviews took place virtually via Zoom, so the participants stayed at their own places and were assessed and interviewed remotely.

Online interviews have benefits and limitations compared with conventional face-to-face interviews. Online interviews provide the researchers with more efficiency, such as reducing travel time and cost, while it also has challenges, including building rapport and online interaction (O' Connor & Madge, 2016). However, the form of interview was the most suitable for me to gather data because it was difficult to conduct face-to-face interviews on campus.

I began by explaining the purpose of the study to elicit background knowledge and build rapport with each participant. If the participants did not provide detailed and in-depth responses, I asked probing questions to enhance their responses. All interviews were conducted in Chinese. After the interviews, I listened to the recordings and transcribed the recordings into a document. Then, I translated the transcription into English. The transcription was saved under an anonymous name.

3.5.2 Assessments

The comprehension assessment was conducted to help understand the participants' perception of their current reading comprehension performance. The assessment explored how Chinese students performed in an IRI's background knowledge, reading comprehension, and reading rate after the time of exposure to an authentic English-speaking environment.

I examined a variety of potential assessments to use in this study and then I located four IRIs that potentially could be used to measure reading comprehension for adolescents or college learners in my study, including Roe and Burns' (2011) *Informal Reading Inventory* (8th Edition) (IRI-RB), Bader and Pearce's (2013) *Bader Reading and Language Inventory* (7th Edition) (BRLI), Brozo and Afflerbach's (2011) *Adolescent Literacy Inventory Grades 6-12* (ALI), and Leslie and Caldwell's (2017) *Qualitative Reading Inventory* (6th Edition) (QRI-6). The TOEFL reading passage was another option for comprehension assessment for college ELs. I determined that the IRI-RB lacked reliability due to the missing reliability figures (Nilsson, 2008), and it was hard to confirm the ALI's reliability without adequate information (Nilsson, 2008). The BRLI was suitable for adult ELs, but the passages were very short, so it was too easy for college ELs. The TOEFL exam was also not a good option, because all Chinese international students had taken the TOEFL before they applied for admission to American universities. So, it was difficult for me to identify a passage that they had never read before as my assessment passage.

I employed Leslie and Caldwell's QRI-6 as the measurement instrument. The QRI-6 is an informal reading inventory, and its purpose is to offer teachers and educators a tool that evaluates and monitors students' reading progress. It can be used to determine students' reading levels, examine individuals' strengths and needs, and document readers' growth. The QRI-6 investigates word decoding, vocabulary knowledge, fluency, and comprehension. The types of passages include narrative and expository texts. The passage lengths vary, and word counts increase while levels increase generally. The reading levels are from pre-primer, primer, first-grade to 12th-grade. Pre-primer and primer levels refer to levels for students who are in kindergarten and at the beginning of the first grade. The first-grade level indicates a level for the first-grade students, and the 12th-grade level means a level for high school students who are in the 12th grade. To achieve construct and content validity, the QRI-6 included "measures of fluency (rate, WCPM, prosody) and comprehension (retelling, implicit questions, explicit questions, and inference questions of various types)" (Leslie & Caldwell, 2017, p. 526). Stories, biographies, social studies, and science text material had been chosen to represent the variety of reading abilities from pre-primer through high school (Leslie & Caldwell, 2017).

Besides, the QRI-6 demonstrated interrater reliability, and "estimates of inter-scorer reliability were found using Cronbach's alpha (Cronbach, 1951). Alpha reliability estimates were .99 for total miscues, .99 for meaning-change miscues, .98 for explicit comprehension, and .98 for implicit comprehension" (Leslie & Caldwell, 2017, p. 531). The QRI-6 showed internal consistency reliability because "Consider the highest SEM for an eight-item test, .18 for 'Wool: From Sheep to You.' A student with a score of 75% has a true score between 57% and 93%, 68% of the time" (Leslie & Caldwell, 2017, p. 532). For test-retest and alternate form reliability, the QRI-6 illustrated "The reliabilities of our instructional-level decisions at all other levels based on comprehension scores were all above .80; 75% were greater than or equal to .90" (Leslie & Caldwell, 2017, p. 536). In addition, the QRI-6 was sensitive enough to detect changes over 10 weeks or longer (Leslie & Caldwell, 2017).

Although the QRI-6 was intended for kindergarten through 12th grade, it was a more appropriate choice than other available IRIs. Some studies have employed the QRI as a measuring instrument to gauge growth in reading (Leslie & Allen, 1999; McKenna et al., 1997; Menon & Heibert, 2005; Sutherland & Neill, 2012; Yeh et al., 2012 as cited in Leslie & Caldwell, 2017). Participants also included ELs, so it could be concluded that the QRI were validated with ELs. As my samples were college ELs, I decided to utilize one high school level passage because the length and content of this passage were similar to the passages of the TOEFL. I piloted two passages with two persons, including the passage about science, and the passage about social studies. They were all native Chinese speakers. One was an undergraduate student who had been here for a year and the other was a graduate student who had been here longer. Both of them had never studied in the U.S. or in English medium schools for K-12. The results indicated that the readers struggled with the passage about science as many biological terminologies hindered them to read and comprehend, while the same readers got better scores with the passage about social studies. Also, this passage had no obvious cultural bias. Thus, the Level 12 passage of World War Ⅰ was appropriate for my participants. The assessment comprised 10 comprehension questions, including 5 explicit questions and 5 implicit questions. "Explicit (literal) questions ask readers to find specific details in the text, while implicit (inferential) questions require readers to combine information from the text and make an inference." (Miller & Smith, 1984) The two types of questions helped examine how readers understood the text. For the assessment section, the participants read aloud the passage and answered the 10 comprehension questions orally. After the assessment, I listened to the recording and calculated the participants' background knowledge, reading rate, and comprehension score (More information on the analysis of the assessment is in the Data Analysis section).

3.5.3 Documents

Document analysis was another data source for this descriptive case study. Yin (2009) explained that documentary information involved all documents that indicated the records of human observations and thoughts, such as books, photographs, essays, etc. For this study, documentary information involved subjects' TOEFL or IELTS scores, the results of the QRI-6 assessment, and their personal statements when subjects applied to American universities.

TOEFL or IELTS scores can show students' English ability, particularly in different language areas: reading, writing, speaking, and listening. The scores give a rough descriptive snapshot of their English ability before they came to the U.S. The QRI-6 assessment illustrates participants' background knowledge, reading rate, and comprehension score. These might demonstrate participants' current reading ability in English.

A personal statement is a compelling statement about prospective students and their interests. It serves as an opportunity to explain to an admissions council how prospective students are uniquely qualified for a specific program in an American university. The personal statements helped my participants to recall their memories and be ready for the retrospective interviews. My participants reviewed their personal statements before the interviews. This served to recreate the context for the period when they had not been exposed to the English-speaking environment and to take them back in time. In this study, I asked the participants to carefully read their written samples before the interviews in order to recall their memories and recreate the context for that period when they prepared their application materials in China. Then they were encouraged to describe their English ability at that time. However, most participants thought they did not need the personal statements to help them recall their memories because they still clearly remembered everything when they first came to the U. S. Actually, the personal statements were not very useful after all. The documents offered lots of data beyond being prompts for the interviews and provided another source to compare the participants' comprehension development in addition to interviews and assessments. All documents were obtained from the participants.

To effectively collect the data, I performed assessments and interviews separately. For the first round of interviews, I asked the participants to take the QRI-6 assessment. The whole process of the assessment was conducted in English. During the second round of interviews, I let the participants look at the writing samples from their applications and then followed up with interviews about their perception. In order to get rich and deep information from my participants, I used our native language, Chinese, to conduct the interviews.

3.6　Data Analysis

The data for this study involved interviews, informal comprehension assessments, and documents. "The data from interviews is a type of qualitative data and researchers aim to extract meaning from it." (Hesse-Biber & Leavy, 2011) The beginning stage of data analysis was to prepare transcriptions. As all interviews were conducted in Chinese, translation was needed. Bryman (2016) provided seven key sequential steps to analyze data from transcribed interviews, such as (1) transcribing the interviews and categorizing groups of relevant statements, (2) coding statements relevant to the experience to identify themes and removing irrelevant expressions, (3) identifying similarities, (4) understanding the meaning of specific expressions, (5) determining textural descriptions of specified categories, (6) using themes, patterns, and categories to create a comprehensive thematic description, and (7) conducting structural synthesis of the perception provided by Chinese international students.

Meanwhile, the thematic analysis was used to analyze the data from TOEFL or IELTS scores, and the QRI-6 assessment results. The thematic analysis emphasized the content of a text and focused on what the text said rather than how it was said (Riessman, 2005). For this study, the two documents might indicate the participants' English ability. Specifically, TOEFL or IELTS scores might represent the participants' English ability in academic literacy, including reading, speaking, speaking, and writing before they were exposed to the ESL context. As well, the QRI-6 assessment results could demonstrate the participants' reading ability in academic literacy, such as background knowledge, reading rate, and comprehension after they were exposed to the English-speaking environment.

The TOEFL/IELTS and QRI-6 scores helped me understand the students' assessed English or reading ability. I compared these scores with the participants' interview responses to find out their connections or disconnections and understand students' perception related to their actual performance. These results helped to answer the third research question: "how does Chinese students' self-perception of their English reading comprehension relate to their actual reading comprehension performance?"

I employed Atlas. Ti v9, a computer-assisted data analysis software tool for the qualitative analysis of textual, graphical, audio, and video data, to assist in the process of identifying meaningful themes, concepts, and descriptions. It assisted me in coding, organizing, and analyzing interview transcripts.

3.6.1 Coding

Codes refer to labels assigning symbolic meaning to the information compiled in a study and they can be used to retrieve and categorize similar data chunks (Miles et al., 2014). Tracy (2013) divided codes into the first-level codes and the second-level codes. The first-level codes represent each idea in the data, examine the data, and assign words or phrases that capture their essence. Also, the first-level codes usually do not need any interpretation (Tracy, 2013). The second-level codes include organizing, synthesizing, identifying patterns, and categorizing them into interpretive concepts (Tracy, 2013). The two levels are usually done in different cycles of coding. In other words, the first-level codes are done in earlier coding cycles, while the second-level codes are done in later coding cycles. Coding is an active process to identify data as belonging to or representing some types of phenomenon (Tracy, 2013).

I employed some fundamental approaches to the first cycle of coding, including descriptive coding, and in vivo coding. Descriptive coding is summarizing data in a word or short phrase. It offers an inventory of topics to index and categorize data. In vivo coding uses the participant's own words or short phrases as codes (Miles et al., 2014).

For example, for the question that asked the participants to describe their friendships in the U. S., I had a code of "friendships". For the question of strategies to learn English, I used a "learning strategies" code.

Then, I cleaned my coding schemes by clarifying, merging, and deleting codes. I clarified codes that were not addressed explicitly, merged codes that were identifying the same thing, and deleted codes that were not working out.

Next, I processed the second cycle of coding, which refers to pattern coding. That is a way of grouping the summaries into a smaller number of categories, themes, or constructs (Miles et al., 2014). In other words, I had to pull together the first cycle of codes into more meaningful and parsimonious units of analysis (Miles et al., 2014). In this study, the second cycle of codes involved challenges, feelings, goals, strategies, and environments. For example, the second cycle of codes of feelings included positive feelings and negative feelings. The code of strategies comprised specific methods and psychology preparation. Additionally, I compared different groups to look for differences, such as females vs. males, undergraduates vs. graduate students, and newcomers vs. people who had been here longer.

I ensured that my study met data saturation because the data repetitions emerged, and no new themes appeared during the data analysis. Meanwhile, theoretical saturation was reached and all relevant information for this study had been found.

3.6.2 Comprehension Assessment

To understand how Chinese students currently performed in the informal reading inventory assessment, I measured the participants' background knowledge, reading rate, and reading comprehension. An oral reading analysis provides insight regarding a reader's background knowledge (i.e. how much a learner knows about the topic), reading rate (i. e. how fast a learner reads), and comprehension (i.e. how well a learner understands the text). Reading rate refers to words per minute (WPM), and it is calculated by dividing the number of words read by the amount of time the reader spends reading the passage.

The comprehension score is calculated by the percentage of correct answers in responses to the comprehension questions. The QRI-6 was used for this procedure. The goal of an informal reading inventory like the QRI-6 is to help teachers identify learners' independent reading level, instructional reading level, and frustration reading level. Being aware of these levels informed me to explore the performance of background knowledge, reading rate, and reading comprehension among Chinese international students in an American university.

There are three reading levels in readers' overall analysis, including the independent level (90%-100% correct), the instructional level (70%-80% correct), and the frustration level (0-60% correct). The independent level refers to the level at which a learner can succeed without any support from others. This is the level at which readers can read fluently with a high level of comprehension. The instructional level provides an estimate of the level at which a learner experiences a mild amount of stress between the text and his/her present reading strategies. At this level, teaching instruction would increase the student's ability to read and understand the text. The frustration level refers to the level at which, even with instructional support, a learner would still have difficulty meeting with success. This is the level at which readers are not fluent and have little memory of textual information. However, each of these levels should be interpreted with caution as Bader and Pearce (2013) indicated that a reader's interest, motivation, and prior knowledge could influence reading levels significantly.

After the assessment, I relistened to the recording and calculated each participant's background knowledge, reading rate, and comprehension score. Also, I created one table for all participants to compare their background knowledge, reading rates, comprehension scores, and overall analysis. More details will be described in Chapter 4.

3.7 Researcher Positionality

As a qualitative researcher, I couldn't separate who I was from my work. My own background and experiences definitely influenced the process of data collection and interpretation. Specifically, my own identity impacted how I reached the participants and how the participants perceived and responded to me so it affected the quality, reliability, and validity of the data I collected. Also, who I was impacted how I interpreted the data. Thus, it was essential to describe my positionality in relation to my research: I was a Chinese international graduate student and a former K-12 language teacher.

When I graduated from university, I became a language teacher, teaching English at one middle school in China. Most of my students began to learn English in middle schools. In China, English language learning is very important for middle school students. Almost all students are required to learn English as a second language for the whole three middle school academic years. English is also one of three major subjects besides Chinese and mathematics. Students must pass the English examination if they want to graduate from middle schools. Most students spend a lot of time in English learning.

After teaching middle school students for ten years, I went to graduate school and worked on my master's degree in teaching Chinese to the speakers of other languages at the top-ranked teacher's university in China. From that moment, I turned into a Chinese teacher. At first, I taught the Chinese language and culture to Western students from the seventh grade through the ninth grade at a British school in Beijing, where students came from different countries all over the world.

In 2009, I first time came to the U. S. as one of 15 participants in the U. S. Teachers of Critical Languages Program, sponsored by the U.S. Department of State and administered by the American Councils for International Education. A Catholic private high school located in Atlanta, Georgia, was my host school. Over this year, I enjoyed using a variety of strategies and activities to create a positive and engaging learning environment. In class, I used Chinese Jeopardy and other games to encourage students to review what they had learned. Outside of class, I set up a tai chi club for students, faculty, and staff to create an opportunity for them to get close to Chinese culture. I also learned a lot from various professional development seminars. In May 2010, my lesson "using kung fu to learn Chinese strokes" was awarded the Best Practice for Foreign Language Teaching by the American Councils for International Education.

After a few years, I became a Chinese teacher through the Confucius Institute at an American university, sponsored by the Headquarters of the Confucius Institutes. First, I began teaching Chinese to college students, faculty, and staff at the university. Then, I moved to an elementary school to teach the Chinese language and culture to students in kindergarten through the fifth grade. Those experiences, at both the elementary school and university levels, greatly enriched my teaching career.

The following August, I came to a public high school, which was described as the "State's most innovative school", and began teaching Chinese to high school students. This school was famous for STEAM, which stood for science, technology, engineering, arts, and math, and the school was grounded in project-based learning and the attributes of teaching next-generation learners. It was also a part of the college of education at a university. Working at this high school made me realize how important it was for teachers to use innovative instructions to stimulate students' thinking and encourage their imagination and creativity.

Due to my unique teaching experiences at various levels from elementary school students to college students, at both public schools and private schools, and in both China and the United States, I felt literacy was my interest. Thus, literacy became my specialization.

Likewise, when I became a Chinese international student, I had a chance to meet with many other Chinese students with a variety of majors. Some were newcomers, while some had been here for years. Some students had confidence in their English, while others were still concerned about their English ability. I was curious how their English proficiencies developed, especially reading comprehension, after they came to the U. S. and were exposed to the ESL context. I was also interested in how an authentic English-speaking environment contributed to their reading comprehension development of academic literacy.

On the one hand, honestly speaking, as a Chinese international student in a second language environment, my identity and experiences impacted my study both in positive and potentially negative ways. First, it brought me a lot of benefits. For example, I shared my first language Chinese with my participants. I did not need translators. We could communicate either in Chinese or in English. We did not have any language and cultural barriers. Those shared characteristics gave me insights and knowledge into their experiences and helped me have a similar perspective as my participants. Also, we had the same experiences as English learners in the ESL context. That provided me with insights into what they were experiencing. It was going to potentially help me to develop a trusting relationship with my participants. The same background as Chinese international students helped me to enhance the trustworthiness of my study. Thus, it made me reach my participants in a smooth way and helped me with data collection. Also, sharing my perspectives with my participants contributed to the interpretation of the data.

On the other hand, being an insider could potentially have drawbacks. For instance, I might have some preconceived notions about what I was going to find because I had experienced or was experiencing some similar things as my participants. I might be relying too much on my own experiences. Those all could blind me in some ways. To mitigate the potential drawbacks, I sought a person who was an outsider to share my data and my findings for a fresh perspective. The outside person I chose was a native English speaker. He had lived in China for about 20 years, and he was proficient in Chinese. He read through my findings and did not provide me with any feedback or suggestion. It seemed like the outside person I found did not help with validating my findings.

However, one of my committee members who was a professor from the Republic of Korea validated my findings. She stated that she had the same perception and experiences as my participants when she was an international student at an American university.

3.8 Summary

This chapter outlined the qualitative research approach, research sample, data sources, data analysis, and my positionality, etc. The qualitative paradigm allowed me to understand and interpret the participants' feelings and thoughts on how an authentic English-speaking environment contributed to their academic reading comprehension. There were 8 participants involved who had different genders, education, exposure time, and majors. Primary data sources for this case study involved interviews, comprehension assessments, and documents. The interviews were conducted in Chinese. The data were analyzed using both data-driven and concept-driven coding.

Chapter 4 Findings

The purpose of this study was to describe and understand Chinese international students' perception of how exposure to the authentic English-speaking environment contributed to their reading comprehension development of academic literacy. In this chapter, the results of the study pertaining to the following research questions were presented and summarized.

RQ1: What perception did Chinese international students have about their English when they were first exposed to the authentic English-speaking environment?

RQ2: How does Chinese international students' initial perception change after years of exposure to the authentic English-speaking environment?

RQ3: How does Chinese international students' self-perception of their English reading comprehension relate to their actual reading comprehension performance?

RQ4: How do Chinese international students perceive the English-speaking environment contributes to their development of academic reading comprehension?

4.1 The Participants

In a qualitative study, researchers seek to investigate a phenomenon by exploring individuals' perspectives and the phenomenon's real-world context (Denzin & Lincoln, 2005). To achieve the goals of this study, I had the opportunity to spend a significant amount of time interviewing the participants about their backgrounds, and experiences of English learning. Through the interviews, I described and understood their thoughts, perception, and experiences regarding reading comprehension development when they studied at an American university. This would not have been possible without the eight participants. I used Student A, Student B, Student C, Student D, Student E, Student F, Student G, and Student H as their pseudonyms to protect my participants' privacy. Below was a brief introduction to students A, B, C, D, E, F, G, and H.

Student A

Student A grew up in a big city in the north of China. She was a Mandarin speaker. She is an undergraduate. She studies at the College of Engineering, and her major is materials and engineering science. She arrived in the U. S. in August 2021, which was 2 months prior to her participation in the study. Everything looks new for her. She will spend 2 years in the U.S., then go back to China to complete her last year for her bachelor's degree. Student A began to learn English in the first grade of an elementary school in China. She also had consistently taken extra-curricular English classes outside the school from elementary school to university. Student A enjoys learning English outside the school. Student A likes to watch some English movies on Netflix, but the movies usually have Chinese subtitles. She listens to English while watching Chinese subtitles. She is open-minded and ready to make some new English-speaking friends.

Student B

Student B grew up in a metropolis in the north of China. He is a Mandarin speaker. He is an undergraduate. He studies at the College of Engineering, and his major is electrical engineering. He arrived in the U. S. in August 2021, which was 2 months prior to his participation in the study. He plans to spend a year in the U.S., then goes back to China to complete his bachelor's degree. He lives with 2 American roommates, and he likes to hang out with his roommates on weekends. They usually go out for playing basketball, doing some shopping, and attending parties. Student B started to learn English in primary school. He relied on self-study, and he thought what he learned in school was useless. He has an accumulation book which is a notebook that records English phrases and words that may be useful in the future. He likes to recite words every day. He watches American TV series in order to accumulate vocabulary and expressions. Also, he likes to communicate with English speakers.

Student C

Growing up in a middle-sized city in the south of China, Student C is a Cantonese and Mandarin speaker, and she began to learn English in primary school. She studies in the College of Arts and Sciences as an undergraduate, and her major is economic management. She arrived in the U. S. in July 2019, which was 2 years prior to her participation in the study. She has some friends who are from Japan, the Republic of Korea, and Nepal. They use English to communicate. Student C will work on her master's program at the College of

Business and Economics after she graduates. In addition to studying here, she works at a Starbucks on campus. Thus, she has some opportunities to communicate with her co-workers and customers in English. She says Cantonese is her mother tongue, so she likes to watch TV series in Cantonese. Also, she enjoys watching English cartoons.

Student D

Student D grew up in a city in the south of China, and he is a Mandarin speaker. He is an undergraduate, and studies in the College of Arts and Sciences with a major in oil painting. He arrived in the U. S. in August 2018, which was 3 years prior to his participation in the study. He likes to make friends, and his friends are also international students. Also, student D works at a cafeteria on campus, and his job is to prepare food and cut the materials into different sizes. He has little interaction with English-speaking co-workers or customers, and he has to spend six hours per day working. He plans to work on a master's program at the College of Business and Economics after he graduates. Student D began to learn English in primary school, and he also used to study English in a private tutoring center to get more practice. He enjoys watching a variety of documentaries online, and the topics involve international politics, finance, economics, sports, and history in both English and Chinese. He regards practicing English as a pleasure.

Student E

Growing up in a small town in southwest China, Student E did not learn English until she was a 6th grader and moved to a big city with her family. She fell behind her peers at that time, and she spent a lot of time in English learning and studied very hard to catch up with them. She is a Mandarin speaker. Now Student E is a doctoral student with a major in chemistry at the

College of Arts and Sciences. She arrived in the U. S. in July 2021, which was 3 months prior to her participation in the study. She is also a teaching assistant in the Department of Chemistry, and she is in charge of a lab section for the course. Student E has many English-speaking friends, and most of them are her classmates who come from Nigeria, Bangladesh, and Sri Lanka. She likes to watch Vlogs online in her spare time because she wants to know how other people live in the world.

Most of them are in English, and their English is quite simple that focuses on daily life. Student E feels a little insecure to use English here, but she is excited to practice her English in an authentic environment.

Student F

Student F grew up in a middle-sized city in the north of China. He is a Mandarin speaker. He began to learn English in elementary school. He had confidence in his English when he was in China as his English achievements at school were always good. Currently, Student F is a doctoral student with a major in chemistry. He arrived in the U. S. in July 2021, which was 3 months prior to his participation in the study. He is also a teaching assistant at the Department of Chemistry. He is in charge of a lab section for the course, and grades students' assignments. Student F feels very nervous when talking on the phone and he becomes worried about his English. He has to pay more time and energy in his teaching job to catch up with his American colleagues. He likes to communicate with his classmates and professors. Student F keeps busy with his study and work and there is little time for entertainment. He believes the environment has a great influence on his English learning.

Student G

Student G grew up in a metropolis in the north of China. She is a

Mandarin speaker. Currently, she is a doctoral student in the College of Medicine with a major in pharmacology. She arrived in the U. S. in August 2017, which was 4 years prior to her participation in the study. Student G spends a lot of time in the lab, and she does not have many opportunities to communicate with other co-workers. She still feels uncomfortable speaking English and she is worried that she cannot clearly express what she wants to express. Student G began to learn English in elementary school. She thinks English in daily life is the most challenging. She cannot understand most of the words her American peers use in daily conversations. That results in her having few American friends. Also, Student G has enormous resistance to English entertainment, and she only watches Chinese TV series.

Student H

Growing up in a small town in the south of China, Student H began to learn English in junior high school. He is a Mandarin speaker. He does not have much confidence in his English, and he thinks it is a little difficult to chat with American students. Thus, he has few English-speaking friends. Student H arrived in the U. S. in August 2018, which was 3 years prior to his participation in the study. He is a doctoral student in the College of Education with a major in education sciences. Also, he works as a teaching assistant in the Department of Educational Policy Studies and Evaluation, and he grades students' homework. Student H likes reading and writing in English specifically. He reads English professional books and articles every day and spends two or three hours per day in English writing. He thinks his English has consistently improved after living and studying in the authentic English-speaking environment.

4.2   Initial Perception about General English and Academic Reading

The participants shared many stories of their time as newcomers, including what their daily routines were, what they did in their personal time, what their first class looked like, and what kinds of interactions they had with their classmates and professors. It was important to note that all participants had general English barriers even though they passed the TOEFL or the IELTS. These language barriers, including oral language, vocabulary, and reading, influenced their daily life and studying directly.

4.2.1   Initial Perception about General English

Although Chinese students had learned English for some years in China, they were still English language learners. Compared with their native English-speaking peers at the university, they were not strong in general English ability. Thus, they met language barriers when they first came here. Student H, who had been here for three years, shared that his experiences when he just arrived here was challenging:

> The first month I came to the United States was very scary. I felt that there was drama everywhere. I felt very nervous because my oral English and listening were poor at that time. When people said fast, I didn't understand what they said. I remembered very clearly that the first time I took a bus, I couldn't take it. There was an American beside me who pulled me to talk. I think he has a very

strong southern accent. I could not understand it at all. Then he said you should go to a language training course. I said yes. I said I could not understand what you were saying.

Student H used words like "very scary" and "very nervous" to describe his initial feelings. His perception of his abilities was like "my oral English ... were poor" and "I didn't understand". Also, Student H mentioned an unnamed American, who told Student H to go to a language training course. Those all contributed to his perception that his English was not good at that time. The American Student H met had "a very strong southern accent". That made Student H realize he could not understand local people's oral language in the authentic English environment. The experiences and feelings described by Student H in this excerpt contributed to the general language barriers he met. This is also an everyday, conversational situation—which usually is considered to be easier language—wise than in academic contexts. These experiences were like disorienting dilemmas for Student H at the beginning of his transformative learning (Mezirow, 1997).

In addition, all participants were concerned about their oral English. Student F was a newcomer and he stated, "The more difficult thing is to express in English. Every time I finish speaking, I feel that the words I use are so 'simple' and 'naive'." Student C had the same opinion as Student F who said, "At that time, when I first came to the United States, my English was very poor." Student A explained, "It's very difficult to speak because there is no language communication environment like abroad in China, and then we don't actually have oral classes in China." This quote was important for my research questions because EFL and ESL learning environments varied.

Students learned EFL in a non-authentic environment, whereas people studied ESL in an authentic environment. Also, EFL classes in China mainly focused on grammar learning, and reading and writing practice. No oral classes were provided. Students had no chance to practice their oral language. Thus, learning English in an authentic environment meant a lot for Chinese students.

Students C, D, E, and G had trouble with listening, and they could not understand what others said when they first came to the U. S. Student E, who was a newcomer to the US, explained, "In terms of listening, I think my listening is not very good, that is, I can understand the standard pronunciation, but for example, if I listen to the listening with an accent, with some accent, and then fast I may not be able to find his keywords." Student E indicated that different English accents bothered her a lot and affected her listening. Her perception was like "I think my listening is not very good". Learning environments were distinct between EFL learning and ESL learning. Learners in the ESL context might be familiar with different English accents.

However, Student D, who had more experience, had a different opinion, and he claimed, "I think it's hard to listen to the news at first because they all speak very fast." Student D could not catch up with the news because of the high speed of the speakers. Student D also stated, "I can't understand it when I watch some American talk shows, as I don't have relatively background knowledge, so I can't understand the point." Background knowledge was important for comprehension. These 2 factors combined made Student D difficult to understand the news and talk shows. In the authentic ESL environment, it is normal for native speakers to speak faster than ELs. I thought both students D and E were right because they were in different stages of exposure to the authentic English environment. Student E was a newcomer. People had a local accent which was very different from what she had learned about "standard pronunciation". Because British English was taught in China and Chinese students used to listen to the British accent instead of the American accent.

Student E still needed time to adapt to the accent, whereas Student D had been in the U. S. for 3 years. I think the fact that he had been here for 3 years helped him to understand that the challenges were about more than accent and speed, but also about cultural and contextual background knowledge.

Student G had been in the U. S. longer and she also had more experience with cultural and context background knowledge. She had the same dilemma as others when she started her Ph. D. program at the College of Medicine. She shared,

> Reading was very difficult for me because I was not good at memorizing words. So, I can't understand the texts very well. Also, my listening was not good … I think the language of life is the most difficult. I mean, for example, talking to people. You have asked me if I have any friends. The reason I have said no is that I can't chat. I think many of the words used in their chat are not understood by me. I mean, but in the chat, they have all kinds of slang or all kinds of jokes and so on, all of which are not understood … Also, my spoken English is very bad.

Student G's perception of her English ability was "was not good" and "very bad". She noted her strugglings with reading and oral language were in large part about the vocabulary. The part about slang and jokes seems really important to the authentic English environment because those things are very local, and hard to teach if you're learning EFL in a non-authentic environment. Student G was concerned more about social language than academic language. Her limited English ability led her to be lonely and not to have English-speaking friends. Student G's experiences were like disorienting dilemmas at the beginning of her transformative learning (Mezirow, 1997). These were also the barriers that international students faced.

Students B, C, and G worried about their English reading, and they had difficulties reading the textbooks. Students C and G had more experience, and Student B was a newcomer. Student B indicated, "Reading depends on the difficulty of the article. If it is a textbook, it may be a little slower. If it is a simple story, it will be a little simpler … Professional vocabulary is difficult, or it depends on what the reading material is." This quote illustrates the participants' initial perception about academic reading comprehension. Textbooks and "a simple story" are largely different. The college textbook is about academic studying in a field and is filled with professional words, structures, and background knowledge while "a simple story" is more like a short and simple narrative story and is easy to read and understand. The participant's use of "professional vocabulary" was connected to terms used in literacy research, such as "content vocabulary", "disciplinary vocabulary", or "academic vocabulary". It seemed like students had difficulties understanding the disciplinary vocabulary and the textbooks when they first arrived here.

My analysis found a difference between undergraduate and graduate students. On the one hand, graduate students perceived they were facing more language barriers than undergraduate students. This may be because graduate students usually had academic jobs like teaching assistants and research assistants, and they had to use more English than undergraduates. For example, as a teaching assistant, Student H helped with grading assignments that were in English. Student G worked in a lab as a research assistant, and she needed to communicate with co-workers and report to the primary investigator regularly. Students E and F were teaching assistants who were in charge of a lab section. They provided presentations for students, answered students' questions, and graded their assignments. Most of their students were native English speakers. Student F stated, "We also have an office hour on Wednesdays, that is, when we go to a learning center, some students will come to ask questions, and then we will answer them how to solve these questions. At that time, we have to speak English for more than three hours." The participants indicated that they were nervous to be required to be professional in a language that was not their own but was the first language of who they were communicating with. As mentioned before, speaking was a challenge for all participants. Speaking academic English for three hours was a challenge for these Chinese international graduate students.

On the other hand, undergraduate students heavily focused on their courses, taking classes, reading textbooks, and doing their homework. Some students had non-academic jobs on campus, like working in the school cafeteria or a coffee shop. They had little time to communicate with co-workers or customers, and even if they did communicate with others, those jobs likely required a more basic, routine range of language. SLA theories and research showed that "everyday" English—English that was used for these kinds of jobs—was a lot easier to master than academic English (Ellis, 2015; Wang, 2016). In addition, based on the participants' perception, undergraduate courses were more commonly lectures, and students had few opportunities to talk with professors and classmates.

Usually, they listened to the lectures, read textbooks, did their homework, took tests, or wrote a final report. It seemed like they gained more receptive skills, including listening and reading, than productive skills, including speaking and writing (Davies, 1976). It also had been shown to have different levels of difficulty for language learners in different contexts.

According to the participants' perception about general English, it could be concluded that (1) the authentic environment played a role in their perception, (2) different contexts in the authentic environment placed different language demands on the students, and those contexts also likely shaped how they perceived their abilities, and (3) factors like different lengths of time might have shaped their perception of when they first arrived. For example, native speakers in an authentic environment usually spoke English fast, had different accents, and liked to use slang and jokes. Working at Starbucks placed different language demands on the student who was a TA. Social language is different from academic contexts. In addition, different lengths of time could shape the participants' perception of their first arriving because students who had been in the U. S. longer had more and deeper understandings of the challenges than newcomers.

4.2.2 Initial Perception about Academic Reading

In addition to the general language barriers, all participants perceived they faced challenges in academic literacy, including (1) learning disciplinary vocabulary, (2) understanding the textbooks, and (3) reading homework and assignments. Student B was a newcomer who shared his challenges in academic literacy:

I don't understand the textbooks because there are a lot of professional words that I haven't touched before, and I have to look them up many times before I can understand them. And many of the words don't correspond to the Chinese meaning, so you have to define something, you can't look up the meaning of the word, it has its own meaning. So you have to read, for example, he writes "helicopter". Even if you look it up in Chinese, you can't understand the definition of it, so this kind of vocabulary is a headache, and it's really huge, and it's this kind of science and engineering textbook, what it writes is not so vivid, not so specific, and it has a lot of abstract things. You shouldn't even understand them in Chinese, and it's really difficult to understand them in English.

Student B's perception of academic reading comprehension was "I don't understand the textbooks", "headache", and "difficult". He met difficulty constructing some academic vocabulary in his field—science and engineering—because these words were abstract and did not correspond to their Chinese meanings. He needed more time to be familiar with them and figure out their meanings. These unknown words also prevented him from comprehending textbooks. Academic vocabulary played an essential role in academic reading comprehension.

Similarly, Student F, who was a newcomer, struggled with reading his homework and assignments, and he claimed,

I think it will be more difficult for me to do homework and assignments. Then it will be more difficult to do the exam. For example, when they have an exam, Americans may spend less than half of the time I have used finishing the whole paper, including reading and writing the answer.

Student F's perception was like "more difficult". He spent more time reading homework and assignments than his American peers. This quote illustrated that the participants needed more time in reading and comprehending homework, assignments, and exams. What Student F was noting was that he actually had less time to answer questions, because it took him a lot longer to read/understand the questions on an exam, compared with his English-speaking peers. This was definitely an equity/fairness issue for English learners.

It was notable that there was one difference between newcomers and people who had more experience. It seemed like people who had been here longer had more exposure to the language and had developed more academic language as a result. They might have also learned/developed more strategies for reading and understanding academic English. Student G had been here longer, and she stated, "It's very easy for me to read academic literature as the vocabulary is very limited. For example, I have read three articles and checked all the unknown words, so there is nothing I don't know." Student G had more exposure to the English environment, and she had developed more academic language. She might also learn more strategies for understanding academic English than newcomers. That could correspond to the stage of Mezirow's transformative learning where they gain new knowledge (Mezirow, 1997).

One thing that deserved attention was all participants in this study felt nervous and insecure to use English when they first arrived here and were exposed to the authentic English-speaking environment. Student F's perception was like "I don't have much confidence, and I think my English is rubbish". Student H perceived English as "very scary", and he was "very nervous". Student C who had more experience had the same negative feelings as others: "At that time, when I first came to the United States, my English was very poor, and now it is also very poor." These experiences were like self-examination with feelings of guilt or shame at the second stage of their transformative learning (Mezirow, 1997). Clearly, the participants had anxiety in the new environment, and they lacked confidence in their English ability. As mentioned in Chapter 2, affective factors such as anxiety and self-confidence may influence readers' comprehension (Kern, 1988). The participants' anxiety and lack of confidence might hinder their reading comprehension in academic literacy.

4.3 Initial Perception Changed over Time

The participants' initial perception about academic reading comprehension changed after different lengths of exposure to the authentic English-speaking environment.

Students A, B, E, and F were newcomers, and they had been in the U. S. for 2 to 3 months prior to their participation in this study. Students C, D, G, and H had more experience and they had studied here for 2 to 4 years before they participated in the study. Students indicated that their reading ability improved, they felt more comfortable with English, and they built self-confidence in using English.

4.3.1 General English Ability Improved

After studying in the English context for a period, the participants thought their general English ability had improved. For example, Student A was a newcomer. When I interviewed her, she just has been here for 2 months. She felt her general English ability had improved a lot, such as oral English, listening, and reading speed. She explained,

I feel my oral English has improved greatly … Then I think listening is the biggest improvement and listening to them [professors and peers] every day makes my listening improve a lot. Then there will be reading, and the speed of reading may be faster than before.

Student A's perception was like "improved greatly", "the biggest improvement", and "improve a lot". It seemed like Student A believed her general English ability improved greatly after a short period of exposure to the authentic English environment.

In addition, Student E who was a newcomer claimed that her listening had improved a lot, as well as her speaking. She believed practice makes perfect. She expressed,

I might improve my listening and oral English. For listening, I could hear it very clearly before, if you were a very standard broadcaster. Now if you change to a person with an accent, I can also think of what he wants to express according to some of his keywords. Then speaking, when you practice speaking, the more times you practice speaking, the more fluent your speaking will become.

Student E's perception was like "more fluent". She also emphasized the different aspects with respect to accents. When she first arrived here, she cannot understand the people with an accent. But now, after three months of exposure to the ESL context, she can understand some. Moreover, her oral English was more fluent because of more practice. These changes showed the authentic environment played an important role in English ability development.

Another newcomer, Student B, claimed the change in his reading ability. He stated,

My reading has improved because I am not used to reading this English at the beginning, but now I read slowly, I can all insist on reading these things in English, and it may get better gradually. My reading improves a lot because I read every day.

Student B's perception changed a lot after exposure. It showed that the participants felt that exposure helped them. Also, student B mentioned strategies he used, like "I can all insist on reading these things in English". He believed that "My reading has improved". Student B believed his reading ability had improved because he had to read academic English daily. For example, he needed to read textbooks, teachers' handouts or PPTs, homework, and assignments. Those consistent and abundant reading practices made his reading ability improve in a short time.

4.3.2 Feeling More Comfortable with English

All participants felt more comfortable with English over time. Student G had studied here for 4 years, and she felt much more comfortable with her English than before. Student G stated,

> I think the words I know in daily life have become more. For example, I adapt to reading English on road signs when I am on the road. If there are eight lanes on a road, I can read the eight blue signs. It was impossible before because that made me have a headache. Regarding other improvements, I think my spoken language seems to have become better than before. Although it is not good enough compared with many people, I feel much more comfortable with my oral English.

When Student G first arrived here, she was not sensitive to English. After immersion for a while, she adapted to the English world. There was a big change between the "before" and "after" part. For example, for talking about her English when she first arrived, she used words like "impossible" and "headache". After 4 years in the English environment, she used words like "adapt" and "comfortable". Student G's perception changed a lot.

She realized her change and was satisfied with it. Now, she felt comfortable with her reading and oral English. It seemed that the environment helped her change. For example, she could not read road signs before the exposure, now she is able to read road signs. The authentic environment made this happen.

Another participant, Student C, had been changed to be comfortable with her reading after living and studying in the U. S. for 2 years. She indicated,

When I first came here, I couldn't understand it at all, because it did not like the IELTS reading, that is, there was a keyword in the topic behind you, and you could probably find the answer according to the word in the text, but my teacher didn't say something and just let me read it. Then I couldn't understand a lot of words in it. When I started to read, I was afraid to read because of so many words I didn't understand. Now, I feel good to read English in class.

Student C's perception changed greatly, from "When I first came here, I couldn't understand it at all" to "Now, I feel good to read English in class". Student G met difficulty in academic reading at the beginning, and she could not understand the disciplinary vocabulary and textbooks. She used "I was afraid to read" to describe her feelings at that time. However, after 2 years of immersion in the authentic environment, her perception changed. It could be concluded that Student C felt more comfortable with English reading than before. Also, Student C took the IELTS classes in China where she had learned a lot of reading strategies and test skills, like "like the IELTS reading ... there was a keyword in the topic behind you, and you could probably find the answer according to the word in the text". These strategies also helped her develop her academic reading comprehension.

As well, Student B who was a newcomer analyzed his change of English. He believed the familiarity made him feel more comfortable using English. He declared, "If I say more, I will naturally become familiar with it. I am familiar with it because I actually know what words to use under what circumstances. This kind of thing is probably known by heart, and then it will come out." Student B's perception indicated that the authentic environment provided him with many chances to practice English. More practice made him more familiar with English. The familiarity let him feel more comfortable with using English.

4.3.3 Building Self-confidence in Using English

All students lacked confidence when they first arrived here, and they were worried and nervous to use English. Also, they thought their English was very poor. But things changed after they had lived here for a while. Students built their self-confidence to use English. For example, Student C stated, "I am thick-skinned now. I'm not worried now. I'm not afraid now. Anyway, if the teacher doesn't understand you, he has to find a way to understand what you're saying." Student C had lived here for 2 years, and she was not worried and was not afraid of using English. She had the confidence to communicate with teachers. In addition, she thought that communication was a two-way street, and the instructor also had a responsibility to ensure communication. The instructor might think about how to communicate with English learners in an effective way, like stating slowly, clearly, and simply. This quote implied the participants changed their initial perception and became confident.

As a newcomer, Student B had studied here for only 2 months prior to his participation in the study. He had a strong feeling about his change. He shared,

> First of all, I think it's confidence. Sometimes I was forced to
>
> say it [something]. But once I said it, I felt that I could say these
>
> words … For example, when I was in English classes before in

college, I stood up to answer questions, my brain began to be confused and I didn't know how to say this in English ... Then I was not confident. Then I came here, and then people talked to you. You were forced to open your mouth, and then you found that you could say something, and then you dared to open your mouth.

Student B's perception was like "forced to" and "dare to". He realized he had a big change in English. He thought the authentic environment forced him to use English daily. That built his self-confidence in using more English in the future. This quote was important for my research questions. It helped us understand the authentic environment changed the participants' initial perception and made them build confidence in using English.

In summary, the authentic English environment contributed to the changes in the participants' initial perception. After immersion for a while, students thought their English ability improved, they felt more comfortable with English, and they built self-confidence in using English. In addition, these experiences suggested the participants were building competence and self-confidence in new roles and relationships at the end of their transformative learning (Mezirow, 1997).

4.4 Perception Related to Actual Performance

This section described how Chinese students' self-perception of their English reading comprehension related to their actual reading comprehension performance. I employed TOEFL/IELTS and QRI-6 scores to help me understand the participants' assessed English or reading ability.

4.4.1 The Participants' Actual Reading Comprehension Performance

Among eight participants, five ones took the TOEFL tests, and three ones had the IELTS tests. The full score of each TOEFL section is 30, and that of each IELTS section is 9. The total points of the TOEFL are 120, and those of the IELTS are 9. The university in the mid-South requires applicant TOEFL scores of 71 or IELTS with 6.0 for undergraduate students and TOEFL scores of 79 or IELTS with 6.5 for graduate students. The range for the participants' TOEFL total scores was between 83 to 98. The range for the participants' IELTS total scores was between 5.5 to 6. The range for the participants' TOEFL readings was between 20 to 28. The range for the participants' IELTS reading was between 5 to 6. Compared with the different groups, it seemed like graduate students had a better performance in reading scores than undergraduate students. Males performed better than females in reading.

TOEFL or IELTS scores might represent the students' actual English ability when they first arrived here, including listening, speaking, reading, and writing. The TOEFL and IELTS examine students' general reading abilities, but they are not necessarily reading comprehension assessments. Meanwhile, QRI-6 scores might demonstrate the participants' current reading comprehension ability. TOEFL/IELTS and QRI-6 scores helped me understand the participants' assessed English or reading ability. I compared these scores with the participants' interview responses to find out their connections or disconnections and understand the participants' perception related to their actual performance. The participants self-reported their TOEFL/IELTS scores. Below is the result.

Table 4.1 The Result of TOEFL/IELTS Scores

Participant	Education Level	Test Name	Listening Score	Speaking Score	Reading Score	Writing Score	Total Score
Student A	Undergraduate	IELTS	6	5.5	6	6	6
Student C	Undergraduate	IELTS	4.5	6	5	5	5.5
Student D	Undergraduate	IELTS	6	6	5.5	6	6
Student B	Undergraduate	TOEFL	15	20	27	21	83
Student E	Graduate	TOEFL	21	22	24	24	91
Student F	Graduate	TOEFL	25	23	28	22	98
Student G	Graduate	TOEFL	23	20	20	25	88
Student H	Graduate	TOEFL	20	18	25	23	86

All eight participants took QRI-6 reading comprehension assessments. As mentioned in Chapter 3, there are three reading levels in readers' overall analysis, including the independent level (90%–100% correct), the instructional level (70%–80% correct), and the frustration level (0–60% correct). The independent level refers to the level at which a learner can succeed without any support from others. This is the level at which readers can read fluently with a high level of comprehension. The instructional level provides an estimate of the level at which a learner experiences a mild amount of stress between the text and his/her present reading strategies. At this level, teaching instruction would increase the student's ability to read and understand the text. The frustration level refers to the level at which, even with instructional support, a learner would still have difficulty meeting with success. This is the level at which readers are not fluent and have little memory of textual information. In addition, a Level 12 passage is a passage that would be expected in 12th grade and below college. Below is the result.

Table 4.2 The Result of QRI-6 Reading Comprehension Assessments

Participant	Length of Time in the U. S.	Education Level	Background Knowledge	Narrative Passage Comprehension			Reading Rate (WPM)	Overall Analysis
				Explicit Question	Implicit Question	Total Question		
Student A	2 months	Undergraduate	8%	80%	100%	90%	93	Independent Level
Student B	2 months	Undergraduate	8%	80%	100%	90%	77	Independent Level
Student C	2 years	Undergraduate	25%	40%	40%	40%	74	Frustration Level
Student D	3 years	Undergraduate	100%	80%	80%	80%	103	Instructional Level
Student E	3 months	Graduate	50%	80%	100%	90%	63	Independent Level
Student F	3 months	Graduate	25%	80%	60%	70%	84	Instructional Level
Student G	4 years	Graduate	50%	80%	100%	90%	93	Independent Level
Student H	3 years	Graduate	33%	60%	60%	60%	86	Frustration Level

For background knowledge, the range was between 8% and 100%. Student D had the highest score, 100%, and students B and A had the lowest scores, 8%. Most students had scores below 50%. That indicated that most participants had inadequate background knowledge of the topic, World War I. Whereas, Student D had adequate prior knowledge about this topic. Also, most people in the group scored between 25% and 50%. That implied the passage I chose would be a neutral topic.

Explicit questions ask readers to find specific details in the text, while implicit questions require readers to combine information from the text and make an inference (Miller & Smith, 1984). The difference examined how readers understood the text. About the explicit questions, six participants out of eight had the highest score, 80% out of 100%, and Student C had the lowest score, 40% out of 100%. That demonstrated most students could be able to recall the text information correctly, while Student C had trouble processing the textual information. Based on the implicit questions, four participants had the highest score, 100%, and the lowest score was 40%. It revealed that most students could comprehend the passage information correctly and make inferences, but Student C had difficulty understanding the textual information.

Comparing the explicit questions with the implicit questions, 4 participants did better in the implicit questions, 3 participants did the same, and a participant had better scores in the explicit questions. That indicated half of the participants could better comprehend the passage information, while Student F could better memorize the text.

Looking across questions, 4 participants answered 90% of questions correctly, and they were at an independent level. That meant they could succeed in memorizing and understanding the textual information without any support from others. 2 participants answered 70%–80% of questions correctly. They were at an instructional level. That indicated they experienced some difficulty in correctly comprehending and memorizing the passage information. At this level, comprehension strategies would enhance their abilities to understand the text. Also, Student H answered 60% out of 100% correctly and Student C had 40% out of 100% correctly. They were at the frustration level. That demonstrated they had little memory of the textual information, and even with instructional support, they might still have difficulty meeting with success.

For the reading rate, the fastest rate was 103 WPM, and the slowest rate was 63 WPM. Reading rates were between 74 WPM and 93 WPM. Bader and Pearce (2013) stated that the reading rates of adult ELs were 80-120 WPM for the beginner's group, 115-133 WPM for the intermediate group, and 120-140 WPM for the advanced group. Therefore, five participants had a beginner's reading rate, and two participants' reading rates were below that of a beginner. That indicated most of the participants experienced some difficulty in smoothly reading the passage, and two of them struggled to correctly read the Level 12 narrative passage.

4.4.2 Perception Matched or Not with Their Actual Performance

I created a table that included information from the previous tables (Table 4.1 and Table 4.2) to help visually represent my findings. Below is the table.

Table 4.3 The Result of TOEFL/IELTS and QRI

Participant	TOEFL/IELTS Reading	QRI Background Knowledge	QRI Total Questions	QRI Reading Rate (WPM)	QRI Overall Level
Student A	6	8%	90%	93	Independent Level
Student C	5	25%	40%	74	Frustration Level
Student D	5.5	100%	80%	103	Instructional Level
Student B	27	8%	90%	77	Independent Level
Student E	24	50%	90%	63	Independent Level
Student F	28	25%	70%	84	Instructional Level

Continued

Participant	TOEFL/IELTS Reading	QRI Background Knowledge	QRI Total Questions	QRI Reading Rate (WPM)	QRI Overall Level
Student G	20	50%	90%	93	Independent Level
Student H	25	33%	60%	86	Frustration Level

5 participants' perception matched their actual performance, including students A, B, C, F, and E. For example, Student F who had been here for 3 months had more positive perception than negative perception about his academic reading comprehension. He had confidence in his reading, and he claimed,

> I think the simplest is reading. I have a strong English foundation. So, my reading is okay including looking at some grammar, looking at complex knowledge structures.

Also, he was satisfied with his reading performance in the TOEFL, and he got 28 points out of 30. He stated, "My reading level was okay, and my reading score was okay, so I had a little confidence in reading." He shared his understandings and strategies on how to improve academic reading comprehension, like:

> I think most of our professional academic English is the translation of some proper nouns, how to describe some professional terms, and how to express some more professional words in English.

When reading the textbooks, pay attention to how the sentences are described in the textbooks.

Student F began to read English literature in his field at his graduate school in China. He had some experience in how understanding or comprehending academic articles and textbooks. He emphasized that disciplinary vocabulary and text structure played important roles in reading comprehension. Additionally, students A, B, and E all had more positive perception than negative perception about their academic reading comprehension. They had confidence in reading, and they performed well in the TOEFL/IELTS reading section and the QRI-6.

Student C who had been here for 2 years, had more negative perception than positive perception about her academic reading comprehension. She had less confidence in her reading comprehension, and she felt academic reading comprehension was more difficult. Also, Student C had poor performance in the IELTS reading and the QRI-6. She had 5.0 points out of 9 in her IELTS reading section. In the QRI-6, she performed at the frustration level, and she only answered 40% of the questions correctly. But Student C's perception matched her actual reading comprehension performance.

3 participants' perception did not match their performance, including students D, G, and H. Student G who had been here for 4 years had more negative perception than positive perception about her academic reading comprehension. She did not have much confidence in her reading comprehension. She used "difficult" or "hard" to describe her feeling. However, her TOEFL reading performance was in the middle of the group. She got 20 points out of 30. She performed well in the QRI-6, and she answered 90% of the questions

correctly. Overall, she performed at the independent level in the QRI-6. Student D had the same situation as Student G. He thought academic reading comprehension was very difficult and had less confidence. But he performed well in the IELTS reading and the QRI-6. He got 5.5 points out of 9 in the IELTS and had 80% of the questions correctly in the QRI-6. Students D and G's perception about reading comprehension was negative, and they thought it was hard.

However, their actual performance was good. Maybe they did not realize their reading comprehension had developed or they were just humble.

Student H thought reading was the simplest compared with listening, speaking, and writing. He also did well in the TOEFL reading and got 25 points out of 30. However, in the QRI-6, he performed at the frustration level, and he answered 60% of the questions correctly. Student H's perception did not match his actual performance, at least in the QRI-6. He explained, "Background knowledge, especially the place names, kind of confused me." Student H's background knowledge score of the QRI-6 was low and just 33%. It seemed like background knowledge and vocabulary played a vital role in academic reading comprehension.

The length of time might have impacted students' scores in the QRI-6. Newcomers seemed to score higher than students who had been in the U.S. longer. 3 out of 4 newcomers, including students A, B, and E, had 90% out of 100%, and their reading levels were the independent levels. Another newcomer, Student F, obtained 70% out of 100%, and his reading level was the instructional level. However, only a participant who had been here longer, Student G, had 90% out of 100%, and her reading level was the independent level. 2 participants, Student C who had studied here for 2 years, and Student

H who had been here for 3 years, had 40% and 60% out of 100% respectively, and their reading levels were the frustration levels. Another participant, Student D who had been in the U. S. for 3 years, had 80% out of 100%, and his reading level was the instructional level. The newcomers had better performance in the QRI-6 than students who had been longer. It could be explained that these students who had here longer had studied in their fields for a long time. They emphasized and developed their disciplinary literacy and paid less attention to other fields. However, the newcomers just completed the TOEFL or IELTS. They had studied and prepared a variety of reading strategies and test skills. That might help the newcomers perform well in the QRI-6.

4.5 Perception about Contributions of the Authentic Environment

In this section, I described how Chinese international students perceived the English-speaking environment contributed to their development of academic reading comprehension. Findings indicated that Chinese students' reading comprehension had improved after exposure to an authentic environment because an authentic English environment (1) was an application environment for English learners, (2) was a rich and valuable resource for English learning, and (3) was a safe and supportive environment that made English learners comfortable with English.

4.5.1 An Application Environment

The authentic English environment provided the participants with an application environment where they must integrate and practice their English in a real context. Student C explained,

When the teacher says something, if you don't understand, you
have to ask the teacher or your classmates in English, and you will
feel that immersion is the forced type, which will greatly improve
your English. It is even better than forcing yourself to speak English
in China.

Student C had studied here for two years, and she used words like
"forced" to describe her experience. She believed the authentic context pushed
her to listen, speak, read, and write in English. She was forced to use English
by circumstances. In addition, Student C pointed out that her English declined
without the application circumstance, and she addressed, "But my English
returned to the original level after I went home and stayed there for two
months." Those all demonstrated that the authentic context played a significant
role in her academic English learning and achievement.

Another participant, Student H, thought the authentic English context
brought some demands or forced him to take the initiative to practice English.
Student H revealed,

So, I think this environment is still very important. I don't like
English very much. That is to say, some people may naturally like
another language. For example, some students in the Foreign
Language Institute like it every day, but I don't like it very much. I'm
more practical. If it doesn't work for me, I may be too lazy to learn
it. So, this kind of environment forces me to learn by myself. It may

be different for others, but I think it is very important for me.

Student H's perception was that the authentic environment "forces me to learn by myself". He was forced to read textbooks, academic articles, and papers. He emphasized his reading had improved a lot after doing this academic work. That indicated the application environment might contribute to his academic reading comprehension.

Student G who had been here longer claimed that the authentic environment was helpful to all aspects of her English, especially reading because she had to see and read English everywhere, such as in the lab she worked. She spent about 8 hours per day in the lab, and everywhere was full of English words in the lab, such as lab instructions, notes, messages, and tags. Student G talked specifically about texts in the environment. These texts that she was encountering were specific to the lab context and made her more familiar with the lab reports and reading. These academic texts would help her with her academic reading and comprehension. Student G pointed out that she became sensitive to English: "The environment has a great influence ... I used to live in the Chinese world. Immersion makes me more sensitive to English now." Student G's experience was typical. She had transferred from the Chinese world to the English world. The authentic environment helped Student G make real-life connections to English. She became sensitive to English words. Familiarity and sensitivity to academic words played a vital role in her academic reading comprehension. Additionally, it seemed like the participants experienced the last stage of their transformative learning and they had a reintegration into their lives based on the conditions dictated by their new perspectives (Mezirow, 1997).

4.5.2 A Rich and Valuable Resource

The authentic environment was also a rich and valuable resource for English learning. It offered students opportunities to communicate with native English speakers or other English learners. Student H stated,

Occasionally I will go to my friends' houses for dinner about once a week or two. They are all native English speakers. So, I learned some English words at that time ... I learn them very quickly.

It seemed like Student H could quickly learn some new words through these communications. Student H not only improved his social English by communicating with native speakers but also improved his academic reading when discussing with his professors or classmates. When asked what helped him with his academic reading, Student H stated that having the class and talking with the professors and peers made him understand some academic words and sentence structures that were commonly used in academics. Those helped him improve his development of academic reading comprehension.

Meanwhile, when asked what strategies helped her with her academic reading comprehension, Student E stated the class she took was a valuable resource because the professor's explanation helped her understand the content of the textbook. She narrated,

Professional words are very strict in science, and words have specific meanings. Just like our biochemistry class, our teacher is a professor with a standard broadcaster accent, he will speak very slowly in class … For example, he said a sentence: "What is the definition of this? " After he said it once, he said sorry, and then he said it again. He just changed one word … He just wanted to express his meaning more rigorously.

Student E's perception was like "very strict in science", "speak very slowly", "just changed one word", and "express his meaning more rigorously". Student E's major was chemistry, and she thought the professional vocabulary in chemistry had a specific and rigorous meaning. Student E's use of "professional vocabulary" was connected to terms used in literacy research, such as "content vocabulary" or "disciplinary vocabulary". If one disciplinary word had been changed, the whole sentence's meaning would be changed. She realized that disciplinary vocabulary was important and might influence her academic reading comprehension. Student E highlighted this experience because she thought the clear and rigorous explanation of the professor helped her understand the content and the textbook. Also, the example of the professor changing one word in the definition reminded her of the importance of discipline-specific words.

4.5.3 A Safe and Supportive Environment

The authentic English environment offered students a safe and supportive environment that could mitigate students' anxiety and build their confidence. Student H talked about the influence of taking part in some activities. He met some nice people, and he experienced a stress-free and friendly environment. That relieved his nervousness and anxiety. As I mentioned before, affective factors, like anxiety and self-confidence, can influence students' English learning and their reading comprehension in academic literacy (Kern, 1988). Student H described,

My friend took me to a place where people read poetry for a long time and were friendly. And they are willing to teach us English. So chatting with them, you can feel more relaxed. Anyway, you can ask any question and they won't mess with you, so they won' t roll their eyes at me. I think this is very good.

Student H's perception was like "friendly", "feel more relaxed", "they won't mess with you", and "they won't roll their eyes at me". That indicated Student H was anxious and nervous when he first came here. He was afraid that people might laugh at him, and he was not confident in himself and his English. Those affective factors could affect his comprehension during the academic reading process. When he realized some people here were friendly and patient, he began to feel relieved. That could help him improve his academic reading comprehension.

Some participants mentioned that professors and peers might help them with their English reading and the academic context. Student C frequently asked her American peers to help with the content when she did not understand the instructor's lecture or textbooks in the class. Student D preferred to acquire some academic feedback from his professors or teaching assistants when he met difficulty reading some professional articles or textbooks. It could be concluded that students felt safe and supported in the authentic environment. This supportive circumstance could relieve students' anxiety and build their self-confidence during the reading process and finally could help students with their development of academic reading comprehension.

4.6 Summary

This chapter described the participants in this study and analyzed the data to answer 4 research questions. First, the participants' initial perception about their general English and academic reading were that (1) they had general language barriers, (2) they faced academic challenges, and (3) they had anxiety and lacked confidence. Second, the participants' initial perception changed over time, including that (1) their general English ability improved, (2) they felt more comfortable with English, and (3) they built self-confidence in using English. Third, regarding the participants' perception related to their actual performance, (1) five participants' perception matched their actual performance, and (2) three participants did not match. Last, the participants perceived that the authentic environment was (1) an application environment, (2) a rich and valuable resource, and (3) a safe and supportive environment.

Chapter 5 Discussion and Conclusion

This study focused on understanding students' perspectives on how an authentic English-speaking environment contributed to their development of academic reading comprehension by analyzing Chinese international students' experience and perception. The study explored the perception that Chinese international students had about their English when they were first exposed to the authentic English-speaking environment, how Chinese international students' initial perception changed after years of exposure to the authentic English-speaking environment, how Chinese international students' self-perception of their English reading comprehension related to their actual reading comprehension performance, and how Chinese international students perceived the English-speaking environment contributed to their development of academic reading comprehension.

Chinese college ELs face numerous barriers to academic success. Students face challenges related to their levels of academic English development of both reading and writing, interactions with American faculty members, and social communication with their peers (Yan & Berliner, 2009; Li et al., 2010). Reading comprehension, a process to extract and construct meaning by interacting with written language, is the most important component of academic literacy (August et al., 2006). International college students typically have smaller vocabularies, less background knowledge of course texts, and less familiarity with mainstream discourse patterns than their native English-speaking peers (August et al., 2006). They also perform more poorly on tests of reading comprehension than their English-speaking peers (Hendricks, 2013).

However, little research has explored Chinese international college students' English reading comprehension development. Likewise, ELs' self-perception of English ability matters to their English achievement. Self-perception of English ability is vigorously shaped by people's experiences. Thus, it is important to understand students' perception of their experiences.

This study was framed by social constructivism theory (Vygotsky, 1978, 1986), sociocultural second language acquisition (Ellis, 2015), schema theory (Tracey & Morrow, 2012), and transformative learning theory (Mezirow, 1997). For sociocultural second language acquisition, Ellis (2015) stated that L2 learning was a process rather than a product because all L2 learning was local and took place in a particular situation.

The language is tied to context and can only be modified or extended in the same or new context. For instance, English learners in the ESL context experience the use of routines and linguistic forms in continuing and authentic English-speaking situations. This is important to my work because Chinese students' English reading comprehension may continue to develop when they are exposed to an authentic English-speaking environment.

Schema theory indicates that "people have schemata for everything in their lives including people, places, things, language, processes, and skills" (Tracey & Morrow, 2012, p. 62), and everyone has individual schemata (Cobb & Kallus, 2011). Anderson and Pearson (1984) asserted readers had schemata for content, reading processes, and different text structures. Developing readers' schemata in the areas of skills and text structures can influence their reading comprehension (Tracey & Morrow, 2012). Thus, Chinese students may develop their schemata for the new reading skills, text structures, and background knowledge after they are exposed to the ESL context. These ultimately can influence their English reading comprehension.

Transformative learning theory introduces the 10 stages of transformative learning to explain how adult learners make sense or meaning of their experiences (Mezirow, 1997). Chinese students might experience some stages of transformative learning, such as a disorienting dilemma and self-examination with feelings of shame when they transferred from the EFL context to the ESL environment. Students who experienced these stages may feel anxiety and lack confidence, which could hinder their reading comprehension development (Kern, 1988). The authentic English-speaking environment would greatly influence their perception of academic reading comprehension. Thus, their perception would be changed over time.

This study used a qualitative research method (Denzin & Lincoln, 2005) and a descriptive case study design (Merriam, 1998) to gain a deeper understanding of how exposure to an authentic English-speaking environment contributed to Chinese students ' reading comprehension development. There were eight participants involved who had different genders (males and females), education levels (undergraduates and graduates), exposure time (less than one year and more than one year), and majors (chemistry, engineering, arts, etc.). Primary data sources for this case study involved interviews, comprehension assessments, and documents. The interviews were conducted in Chinese, and they used open-ended interview questions that aligned with research questions, such as "What has helped you to feel more comfortable with English".

For the reading comprehension assessment, I employed the Level 12 passage on World War I of the QRI-6 (Leslie & Caldwell, 2017) to help understand the participants' perception of their current reading comprehension performance. The assessment comprised 10 comprehension questions, including five explicit questions and five implicit questions. The participants read aloud the passage and answered the 10 comprehension questions orally in English. I calculated each participant's background knowledge, reading rate, and comprehension score. Documentary information involved subjects' TOEFL or IELTS scores, and the results of the QRI-6 assessment.

I employed thematic analysis to analyze the data from TOEFL or IELTS and QRI-6 scores. TOEFL/IELTS and QRI-6 scores helped me understand the participants' assessed English or reading ability. I compared these scores with the participants' interview responses to find out their connections or disconnections. These results helped to answer the third research question.

The findings answered all four research questions. First, the participants' initial perception about their general English and academic reading were that (1) they had general language barriers, (2) they faced academic challenges, and (3) they had anxiety and lacked confidence. Second, the participants' initial perception changed over time, including that (1) their general English ability improved, (2) they felt more comfortable with English, and (3) they built self-confidence in using English. Third, regarding the participants' perception related to their actual performance, (1) five participants' perception matched their actual performance, and (2) three participants did not match. Last, the participants perceived that the authentic environment was (1) an application environment, (2) a rich and valuable resource, and (3) a safe and supportive environment.

5.1 Discussion

Above I described the participants' initial perception about general English and academic reading, how their initial perception changed over time, their perception related to actual performance, and their perception about the contributions of the authentic environment. Findings also demonstrated some factors that the participants perceived affected their development of academic reading comprehension.

5.1.1 Factors That Influenced the Participants' Reading Comprehension

5.1.1.1 Academic Vocabulary

The professional vocabulary my participants talked about is usually referred to in literacy as academic vocabulary, which can be divided into general academic vocabulary and content-specific or discipline-specific vocabulary. 6 participants thought academic vocabulary was essential for their English academic reading comprehension. Student C felt academic reading comprehension was more difficult because of a lot of vocabulary she did not know. She explained, "I think the biggest difficulty is the vocabulary because if you can't understand the words, you can't understand what it is saying ... The vocabulary affects my understanding of the article." Student D thought academic articles were very difficult and depended on whether they knew enough of the vocabulary. The participants perceived discipline-specific vocabulary as a foundation for academic reading. The participants who had more words might better comprehend the text.

Student B indicated academic words prevented him from understanding the textbook and he reported,

I don't understand the textbook, there are a lot of professional words that I haven't touched before, and I have to look them up many times before I can understand them. And many of the words don't correspond to their Chinese meanings, so you have to define something, you can't look up the meaning of the word, it has its own meaning.

Student B indicated that Chinese translation could not help him understand these discipline-specific words like "mortise" and "tenon" because they were abstract. He even did not know the definition in Chinese. Student E met the same obstacle in disciplinary vocabulary, and she declared,

The discipline-specific vocabulary is very difficult for me ... because the word is a patchwork, it has a prefix and a suffix, and then the middle piece may also be a very difficult word, it may also be from Latin, then from French, and it's also a foreign word, and it's not easy to read.

Student E was a doctoral student, and her major was chemistry. Her quote indicated two things: morphology (the structure of words) and word etymology (the origin of words). She thought the discipline-specific words in chemistry were difficult to learn because the structures of these words were complicated involving prefixes, roots, and suffixes, and she was also not familiar with the history of words. Morphology helps readers to have a better and more thorough understanding of words (Miller & Veatch, 2010). Additionally, research showed that more than 60 percent of all English words had Greek or Latin roots, and in the vocabulary of the sciences and technology, the figure rose to more than 90 percent (Green, 2020). Those demonstrated that morphology and etymology played a role in academic language and studying morphology and etymology could help students better understand professional words and increase reading comprehension.

Student E also shared her solution of how to learn English disciplinary vocabulary. She expressed,

I need to translate it into Chinese on the Internet. I just knew that it meant this, and then I used my previous knowledge to give the meaning of the English word ... I will learn the new things in the Chinese textbook and then go back to see what they said in English. I think this will make me understand faster.

Student E stated this translation way worked well for her, and she could understand the discipline-specific words and textbooks fast. She used her first language and previous knowledge of the subject to scaffold her second language reading comprehension.

Moreover, another participant, Student G had been here for 4 years and experienced how disciplinary vocabulary affected her reading comprehension. Before Student G went to the U. S., she took the TOEFL and claimed, "Reading was very difficult for me because I did not memorize words. So, I can't understand the texts very well." Student G got 20 points out of 30 on her

TOEFL reading test. It made sense she had these feelings. It looked like the shortage of vocabulary hindered her academic reading comprehension.

Student G experienced challenges during her first academic school year and she stated, "English academic vocabulary was too hard in my first year … I couldn't understand the questions at all in some exams, so I couldn't answer them correctly, which was a big problem." After the first year, she mastered most of the academic vocabulary related to her field. Student G changed her opinions and declared, "It's very easy for me to read academic literature as the vocabulary is very limited. For example, I have read three articles and checked all the unknown words, so there is nothing I don't know." It seemed like Student G could easily understand academic articles in her field after she learned most academic words. The academic vocabulary helped her better comprehend the texts. Student G's experiences indicated that academic vocabulary was a basic element for academic reading comprehension, and it played a crucial role in the process of academic reading.

In addition, Student A pointed out that academic vocabulary influenced her academic reading comprehension. She claimed,

At the very beginning, there were many academic words in the major course of materials. Those words were very long and difficult to read. I looked them up in the dictionary, and I was not able to remember them after the first time. Then, I tried again, and I failed to remember them again. In addition to these major courses, other courses, such as mechanical engineering, emphasized calculation instead of theory. That is relatively easier to understand because it does not have so many academic words … Sometimes I may encounter some unknown keywords when I read the questions that make me not comprehend the meaning of the question.

Student A's major was materials and engineering science and she had been here for 2 months. She claimed that terminologies were long and difficult to read, and it took her a lot of time to remember and understand them. These experiences were like the acquisition of knowledge and skills for implementing her plans at the seventh stage of transformative learning theory (Mezirow, 1997). Also, Student A's perception revealed that disciplinary vocabulary was important for academic reading and comprehension. Discipline-specific vocabulary in materials and engineering science might be very different from Chinese terms. Student A was just a newcomer. She might need more time to be familiar with them and understand them.

5.1.1.2 Background Knowledge

3 participants mentioned that background knowledge was crucial for their academic reading comprehension. Student C believed background knowledge was important for comprehension, and she stated, "Because of the academic and professional differences, it does not really reflect my actual English ability. If it is related to my major, I may do better." Student C seemed confident to have a better performance if the materials were related to her field because she thought her background knowledge about her major could greatly help with academic reading comprehension.

Another participant, Student H, had much confidence in his academic reading comprehension. His major was education sciences. However, he performed poorly in the QRI-6. He explained that was all because of a lack of background knowledge, and he related,

Background knowledge, especially the place names, kind of confused me ... All kinds of place names were strung together, especially there were several countries that I had never heard of ... I was a little confused when I answered the questions ... I don't understand World War I, and if you change to World War II, the score may be a little higher ... If you choose another topic like biology or biomedicine, I'm afraid the score will have to be decreased a little more.

Student H stated that his performance was not good because he lacked background knowledge of World War I and if he had adequate previous knowledge, he would perform much better. Student H emphasized background knowledge was essential for academic reading comprehension.

Additionally, Student D was the only participant who scored 100% on the background knowledge portion of the QRI assessment. His major was arts with an oil painting specialization. He clarified background knowledge helped him with comprehension, and he added, "But I also think it depends on the situation. Because, how to say, like some natural science articles, I can't understand anything. I think the difficulty of this article is a little above the middle, but it is not difficult." Student D's perception reinforced that background knowledge played an important role in academic reading comprehension. Student D enjoyed watching a variety of documentaries online, and the topics involved international politics, finance, economics, sports, and history in both English and Chinese. His interests enriched his background knowledge in different fields and also helped him with comprehension.

5.1.1.3 Reading Aloud

Some students indicated that reading aloud by themselves impeded understanding the text. Student F expressed that reading aloud blocked his comprehension, and he explained his opinion:

> When I am reading English, I don't know how to describe it. Anyway, when I read English, I want to read a little faster, and I want to try to pronounce it in a standard way. So, in the process of reading, when I read orally, I may neglect some understanding and feeling of the sentence, and also neglect some memory of what the whole article is about because I will pay more attention to how to read the word, how to read the sentence, how to break the sentence and so on. It is a kind of neglecting memory and understanding.

Student F's perception indicated that reading aloud or orally influenced his comprehension. He put more energy and attention into pronunciation so that he could not remember much information about the text, and he could not understand the text well. It seemed that reading orally distracted his comprehension. Student F's reading rate was 84 WPM, and he was in the beginner's group (Bader & Pearce, 2013). That indicated he experienced some difficulty in smoothly reading the passage. Research showed that reading fluency played an important role in comprehension and fluent readers were better able to comprehend the text because automatic word reading supported their abilities to stay focused on the text's meaning (Yeh & Inose, 2003; Pikulski & Chard, 2005; Williams et al., 2011).

When I was doing the QRI-6, the participants were asked to read the passage out loud. Student E also thought reading orally hindered her comprehension, and she stated, "When I read that article, I feel that when I read it out, it is stumbled, but if it is not read aloud and just look at its meaning, it is actually quite simple, though there are some new words." Student E's perception demonstrated that reading aloud blocked her process of reading and she could perform better if reading silently. Both students F and E's perception emphasized that reading aloud discouraged their comprehension during the reading process.

5.1.1.4 Strategies

The participants pointed out that reading strategies were critical for academic reading comprehension. When Student G was speaking specifically about the QRI passage, she related,

> I feel that I don't understand a lot of the content when I read it. But it seems that you can answer these questions without understanding them. I still don't know what World War I is all about.

Student G did not understand the text, but she answered 90% of the questions correctly. She correctly answered 80% of the explicit questions and 100% of the implicit questions. Connected to the study of Keenan and Betjemann (2006) in Chapter 2, Student G's performance was familiar to these native English-speaking undergraduates who were able to answer 86% of comprehension questions correctly without reading the passages of the Gray Oral Reading Test. It could be explained that Student G had learned a lot of reading comprehension strategies like these native English speakers, including (1) re-reading the text, (2) activating prior knowledge, (3) using context clues,

(4) locating keywords, (5) making predictions (Almasi & Fullerton, 2012). And Student G did well in using these strategies, and she mentioned, "In my opinion, it was just going back to the article to find the same word as my most frequently played game, matching the same picture." It seemed like she employed one reading comprehension strategy—locating keywords. Thus, it seemed that reading strategies played an important role in academic reading comprehension.

5.1.1.5 Affective Factors

Generally, my participants experienced the beginning stages of transformative learning theory when they first came to the U. S. They had a disorienting dilemma and self-examination with feelings of guilt or shame (Mezirow, 1997). These experiences made them feel anxious and unconfident. It was notable that the participants' affective factors, including anxiety and lack of confidence, might hinder their reading comprehension in academic literacy. Student E emphasized affective factors were considered for her reading comprehension, and she claimed, "I think the affective factors are very important when I do some reading. If I feel relaxed, then I can read very carefully."

Student E's perception was like "the affective factors are very important" for the reading process. When readers felt relaxed, they could read carefully and put more energy into reading and comprehension. That made sense because anxiety and self-confidence could influence readers' comprehension (Kern, 1988). That confirmed that affective factors also played a critical role in academic reading comprehension.

5.1.2 Unexpected Findings

It was notable that the length of time the participants had been in the U.S. might impact their scores in the QRI-6. Newcomers seemed to perform better in the QRI-6 than students who have been in the U. S. longer. This is an unexpected finding—we might expect that people who have been here longer would do better. It could be explained that these students had studied in their fields here for a long time and they spent much more time in their disciplinary literacy. However, on the one hand, the QRI-6 passage was not related to their discipline, and they may not have enough background knowledge or disciplinary vocabulary. On the other hand, the newcomers just completed the TOEFL or IELTS tests. They were more familiar with a variety of reading strategies and test skills, such as re-reading the text, activating prior knowledge, using context clues, locating keywords, and making predictions (Almasi & Fullerton, 2012). Those might help the newcomers perform better in the QRI-6.

In addition, graduate students might face different language challenges or expectations compared with undergraduate students. On one side, Students E and F were both graduate students and they perceived they needed to improve their oral English because their TA jobs had high expectations or requirements for speaking and communicating with students, colleagues, and professors. Student H, who was a graduate student, thought academic writing was very important and difficult. He spent a lot of time reading and writing every day because it was necessary for his RA job and academics, including grading, final reports, dissertation, and publications. On the other side, students A, B, and C were undergraduate students and perceived they had few chances to speak with classmates and instructors. They spent a lot of time to read the textbooks, handouts, and instructors' PowerPoint Slideshows (PPTs) in addition to listening to instructors' lectures. Listening and reading were crucial for their academics. Students C and D who were undergraduates stated their campus jobs were labor jobs and they did not need to talk with others often during their work. Therefore, undergraduates experienced much more receptive language skills, like listening and reading. In addition to these receptive language skills, graduates were expected to have more expressive language skills, such as speaking and writing. Also, graduates' expressive language relied on a much more sophisticated level of reading comprehension, including critique and synthesis, rather than the low-level identification or inference that the TOEFL or the IELTS requires. Thus, graduate students might perceive more difficulties because they were required to have high-level language skills in both receptive and expressive language.

5.2 Implications

This study was important because it (1) explored the perception of Chinese international students related to their academic reading comprehension, which was an area where not much research currently existed, and (2) explored how the authentic English environment impacted the students' perception, and (3) explored how the implications of immersion could impact the students' development of academic reading comprehension.

Additionally, the findings of this study might be generalized to other international student groups. For example, there may be more similarities between Chinese, Japanese, and Korean cultures, so there might be similarities in education and culture. The findings could be effectively generalized to

Japanese and Korean international students. But it is hard to generalize these findings to the international student groups whose official language is English, such as Indian, Pakistani, Sri Lankan, etc., because these students have already been exposed to an English-speaking environment in their home countries before they go to the U. S. The authentic English circumstance is not new for them, and they may not be sensitive to the change anymore. Moreover, the findings may apply to students from other places that are not Asian and not English-speaking because they have many similarities with Chinese students, such as first exposure to the authentic English-speaking surrounding, different home languages, and educational or cultural discrepancies.

5.2.1 Implications for Practice

This study may help higher education institutions and instructors better understand and support Chinese international students ' academic English development. For example, the university where this study occurred offers English learners some programs, such as adult ESL classes, a semi-intensive English program, and an international conversation hour. Adult ESL classes sponsored by the university allow students to practice conversation and pronunciation. Participants can learn vocabulary, phrases, and American slang. The classes are free and available to the university's J-1 visiting scholars, J-2, F-2, and H-4's spouses. However, the free classes are not served to the F-1 international students. Thus, most Chinese students are not eligible for the course. Also, the classes do not focus on academic English, so they're hard to improve Chinese students ' academic English development. The university could allow the F-1 students to participate in these courses or develop ones specifically for them to support these students.

In addition, the semi-intensive English program sponsored by the Center for English as a Second Language (CESL) aims to improve the general language skills of English learners and focus on listening, speaking, reading, and grammar. This course can help Chinese students with their academic literacy. However, the course is not free, and students have to pay tuition. Thus, students may not participate in it due to the charge.

The international conversation hour is a free on-campus resource for those who are willing to practice daily, conversational English and meet international and U.S. students. This kind of ESL course can help Chinese students with their oral English and also help students feel more confident in interacting and socializing with their native English-speaking peers. Also, a free course in academic reading is strongly needed which is intended to improve students' academic English development by providing students with specific English reading strategies. These classes should be geared toward different disciplines. That means students in the sciences need different academic reading skills and strategies than students in the arts or social sciences based on different discipline-specific practices (Fang & Coatoam, 2013). In addition, students from different disciplines need to emphasize discipline-specific vocabulary because 6 out of 8 participants confirmed disciplinary vocabulary was essential for academic reading comprehension. Also, students are encouraged to enrich their background knowledge related to their fields and improve their English reading strategies.

A tutoring center may offer services to support students' writing and improve their academic writing abilities. Although most universities already have tutoring centers and/or writing centers, tutors need to have training in working with English learners. For example, tutors should realize international students come from different educational backgrounds and have different

cultural backgrounds and language abilities. That means every student has
individual schemata (Cobb & Kallus, 2011), and developing readers' schemata
in the areas of skills and text structures can influence their reading
comprehension (Tracey & Morrow, 2012). According to the findings of this
study, Chinese international students have general language barriers, face
academic challenges, and have anxiety and lack confidence. Tutors may slow
the pace of instruction or delivery, increase wait time, and create a safe and
supportive environment. Also, the office for international students can organize
activities to help students involve in campus life and make connections with
American peers or students from other countries. To better serve students, the
office may hire some native English speakers and assign each English speaker
a small group of international students or English learners to help them learn
about U.S. culture, practice English, and develop cross-cultural communication
and mediation skills to help students build schema, and also help international
students develop academic/disciplinary vocabulary that could help them in
their academic reading.

Instructors are recommended to communicate with their Chinese students
and understand their difficulties with the courses. Likewise, institutions should
provide instructors with training or support on how to help international
students successfully transfer to American classes, and how to teach them
effectively and help them with their academic development. Also, instructors
should clearly state their expectations for Chinese students and help them
know the cultural expectations of the US classrooms.

Based on my research findings, there are some strategies that my
participants identified as particularly helpful to their academic reading
comprehension, such as emphasizing disciplinary vocabulary, preparing enough

background knowledge, and learning important reading strategies. Moreover, instructors may engage Chinese students in the class by asking them questions, putting them in group work, and offering them chances to express their thoughts or opinions.

In addition, the graduate students who are TAs might have extra needs than undergraduate students and graduate students who are not TAs. TAs are expected to have better abilities in English listening and speaking in order to efficiently communicate with their students. They play a big role at the university, and many of them are going to stay in academics and continue to sharpen their English skills. As teachers, TAs have to be very sensitive to nuance. It is difficult for non-native speakers to pay attention to nuance and "read" what is unsaid. What is not said is critical sometimes. Thus, TAs are expected to develop a variety of skills in both language and teaching. Also, L2 oral proficiency could support L2 reading ability (Wang & Koda, 2005; Koda, 2007). Moreover, students whose perception does not match their current performance may consider building their confidence in their English ability and reinforcing their background knowledge based on the findings of this study.

Likewise, using the same assessment for undergraduate and graduate students may not be appropriate. As I mentioned before, undergraduates experienced more receptive language skills (listening and reading), while graduates were required to have more expressive language skills (speaking and writing). However, the TOEFL and IETLS are still major admissions tests for most American universities. In addition to the total scores of the TOEFL or IELTS, college admission may emphasize students' listening and reading scores, and graduate school admission should consider focusing on speaking and writing scores. In order to better know what students' abilities are, college admission may provide undergraduate students with extra listening and reading assessments, whereas graduate school admission could require graduate students to take additional oral language and writing tests. It is essential to note that silent reading tests are more appropriate because the findings illustrated that reading aloud discouraged the participants' comprehension during their reading processes.

5.2.2 Implications for Future Research

Previous research indicated the importance of reading comprehension in academic literacy and disciplinary literacy at the college level, but in most studies, researchers did not state whether participating students were native English speakers or L2 learners. As we know, L2 learners have difficulties in academic contexts, including engaging in a variety of academic and social practices and negotiating multiple academic discourses in various circumstances (Curry, 2004; Lei et al., 2010). However, it is rare to find research that emphasized L2 learners' academic reading comprehension development. It would be helpful to have studies that had pre-post designs, and/or that followed students across a year or more to see how the environment contributed to their academic English comprehension. More research on that topic will be needed in the future.

L2 reading comprehension is more complicated than L1 reading comprehension, and it also depends on learners' L1 reading ability and their L2 oral proficiency (Bernhardt, 2005; Wang & Koda, 2005; Koda, 2007). Due to the large L1–L2 orthographic distance between English and Chinese, Jiang (2011) argued that L1 reading ability predicting L2 reading may not apply to Chinese L2 learners. It probably reveals that oral proficiency in L2 is more important. However, more evidence is still needed to confirm that and future research on that topic should be done.

Research still needs to explore the specific strategies for Chinese international students. The study has shown that teachers could utilize reading strategies to improve adult L2 learners' reading comprehension and academic achievement, whereas some reading strategies that teachers employed (e.g. vocabulary pre-teaching, comprehension question presentation) had fewer effects on Japanese adult L2 learners' reading comprehension (Mihara, 2011). However, it is unclear if and how these reading strategies affect Chinese international students' reading comprehension, and thus more research is needed.

In addition, the TOEFL and IELTS are the two major assessments for international students, but they are not necessarily reading comprehension assessments. Although Chinese students successfully passed the tests to gain entrance to U. S. institutions, they still encounter difficulties with comprehension in specific disciplines. We still need to learn how specific disciplines impact international students' comprehension, as well as how to support students' comprehension in those disciplines. Research on that topic should be done next to help students succeed in international higher education.

Oftentimes, people assume that math and science are easier for English learners, because "numbers are the same" and "the concepts are the same". However, there is research showing that this is not true (Hill & Kathleen, 2006; Laplante, 1997). Student B's quote also challenges that assumption. His perception of academic reading comprehension was "I don't understand the textbooks", "headache", and "difficult". He met difficulty constructing some disciplinary vocabulary in his field—science and engineering—because these words were abstract and did not correspond to their Chinese meanings. He needed more time to be familiar with them and figure out their meanings.

These unknown words also prevented him from comprehending the textbooks. Student B's perception may confirm some research that shows that math and science are the hardest for ELs (Hill & Kathleen, 2006; Laplante, 1997). More research on that topic should be done in the future.

There are still gaps in research that need to be addressed. Although we know how various factors affect Chinese students' comprehension and academic success in general, we do not know how disciplinary literacy and comprehension interact for Chinese international students. Specifically, a Chinese student majoring in engineering might have different experiences than one majoring in psychology. Many English terms in engineering may block Chinese students from comprehending the textbooks, while a lack of background knowledge in Western psychology may make Chinese students have difficulty understanding the textbooks. Emergent design can be used for this study as qualitative researchers think the research process is emergent (Creswell, 2009).

The participants may include two groups of Chinese students, one group majoring in engineering and the other group majoring in psychology. "Since the initial research plan cannot be prescribed, all phases of the process may change or shift after the researcher begins to gather data." (Creswell, 2009) The purpose of this study was to learn about the problem or issue from the two groups of students and to understand how different disciplinary literacy and comprehension interacted for Chinese students.

Moreover, students with different social or economic backgrounds might encounter different obstacles. For example, students from higher socioeconomic families who have the means to travel overseas or hire a native speaker tutor have more opportunities to practice their oral English with native English speakers than their peers from lower socioeconomic families. Thus, spoken English is less of an obstacle for them. The theoretical lens may be recommended for this study (Creswell, 2009), in order to view how socioeconomics plays a role in English reading and comprehension development among Chinese students. Future research on these topics might be encouraged.

5.3 Limitations

Likewise, some limitations existed for this study. First, in qualitative research, the researcher is the instrument for both data collection and interpretation. Thus, my background and experiences might have influenced the process of data collection and interpretation both in positive and potentially negative ways. Obviously, my positionality brought me a lot of benefits, including no language and cultural barriers, easily developing a trusting relationship with my participants, helping me with data collection, and contributing to the interpretation. Being an insider could potentially have drawbacks, such as relying too much on my own experiences, and blinding me in some ways. To limit those biases, I continuously engaged in reflections, provided transparent reports to reveal a personal bias, and asked outsiders to check the transcript and interpretation. However, it was hard to get outside researchers to review my data and findings. The outsider I chose did not offer any feedback, so he did not help with validating my findings.

Next, all data in this study was self-reported, except QRI-6 scores. Thus, I assumed the participants responded truthfully. Likewise, the QRI-6 passage I selected might have a limitation. I picked the passage of World War I because it seemed not to have a cultural bias, but some of my participants were not familiar with the history and they did not have enough background knowledge of this topic. That also confirmed the study of Huang (2012) in Chapter 2, which stated that Chinese students were not familiar with the learning materials of the social sciences because these materials were more likely relevant to American culture or history, so Chinese students may have to spend more time and make more efforts to synthesize information. But the findings of this study indicated the participants' background knowledge might not influence their QRI-6 scores as some students with low background knowledge obtained high QRI-6 scores. Also, the QRI-6 is not commonly used for college English learners so that it has implications for limitations.

Additionally, the recruitment of the participants might have a limitation. I planned to recruit 8 participants who had varied majors. However, two of my participants had the same major, chemistry. That might slightly influence my findings. Last, I reasonably believed I reached theoretical saturation, though it is also possible that a somewhat larger sample size might have made my findings more solid.

5.4 Summary

This chapter summarized the whole study including the purpose, theoretical framework, methods, data sources, and results. It also provided implications for practice and future research. This study is important for U. S. institutions, instructors, and students. More research on some specific topics might be encouraged to be done in the future. In addition, this chapter demonstrated some limitations which existed during the process of data collection, data analysis and interpretation, and the recruitment of participants.

Appendices

Appendix 1 Interview Protocol English Version

Research on Chinese international students' development of reading comprehension in an English-speaking environment: A descriptive qualitative study

1. Before the interview, the participants will be asked to review their writing samples from their applications to help them answer interview question 7.

2. The participants will also be asked to look at their TOEFL or IELTS scores and answer the question about them in the interview.

3. Explain the purpose of the study to each participant at the beginning of the interview.

4. Review the informed consent release form with each participant and answer any questions the participants may have.

5. Obtain a verbal agreement to record the interview session by video.

6. Each participant will have a pseudonym based on their experiences.

General Background Questions

1) Please tell me your name, gender, and age. Are you an undergraduate student or a graduate student?

2) Tell me about your college, academic program, and major.

3) How long have you studied at the University of Kentucky?

4) Could you describe your friends at the University of Kentucky? For example, are they mostly Chinese speakers? Do you have American friends or other English-speaking friends?

5) When do you watch TV or movies? What language are the programs? Why do you choose those programs?

6) How many hours per day do you spend using English, including your academic study and your entertainment?

Questions about Initial English

7) Tell me about learning English before you came to the U. S. For example, where did you learn English? What were the classes like? What parts were easy for you? What parts were hard for you?

8) When looking at your writing sample from your application, how did you feel about your English ability before you came here?

9) You are looking at your TOEFL or IELTS scores, please talk about how those scores and how you think about your performance on the test. Can these scores reflect your actual English ability at that time?

10) How well prepared did you feel to use academic English at the University of Kentucky?

11) What was easy and what was difficult in using English to study here?

Current English Perception

12) After studying at the University of Kentucky, how do you feel about your English ability now? What has been improved?

13) How did you overcome the challenges specific to English in your academic study?

14) These are your QRI scores, how do you think about these scores and what do you think about your performance now?

15) Do you think these scores can reflect your actual English ability?

16) What has helped you to feel more comfortable with English?

17) What kinds of things do you do to support yourself in continuing to learn English?

18) Is there anything else you would like to share with me about your English learning?

7. Transcribe the interview recordings in a verbatim format and remove any verbiage that may lead to recognizing the participants or organizations. The transcriptions of the interviews will provide a record for the data analysis.

Appendix 2 Interview Protocol Chinese Version

英语环境下中国留学生阅读理解能力发展的论文研究：
描述性定性研究

1. 面试前，参与者将被要求查看他们申请中的写作样本，以帮助他们回答面试问题 7。

2. 在面试中，参加者还会被要求查看他们的托福或雅思成绩，并回答相关问题。

3. 在访谈开始时向每名参与者解释研究的目的。

4. 与每名参与者一起查看知情同意书并回答参与者可能提出的任何问题。

5. 获得同意对访谈会话进行录音的口头协议。

6. 每名参与者将根据他们的经历使用化名。

一般背景问题

1) 请告诉我你的姓名和年龄。你是本科生还是研究生？

2) 告诉我你的学院、你的学术项目和你的专业。

3) 你在肯塔基大学学习了多久？

4) 你能描述一下你在肯塔基大学的朋友吗？例如，他们大多是说中文的吗？你有美国朋友或其他说英语的朋友吗？

5) 你什么时候看电视或电影？这些节目使用的是什么语言？你为什么选择这些节目？

6) 你每天使用英语的时间有多少（包括你的学习和娱乐活动在内）？

关于初始英语的问题

7）谈谈你来美国之前学习英语的情况。例如,你是在哪里学的英语? 课程是怎样的? 哪些部分对你来说很容易? 哪些部分对你来说很难?

8）在看到你申请中的写作样本时,你来这里之前对你的英语能力有什么看法?

9）你现在看到的是你的托福或雅思成绩,请谈谈这些分数如何,以及你如何看待你在考试中的表现。这些分数能反映你当时的英语水平吗?

10）对于在肯塔基大学使用学术英语,你准备得充分吗?

11）在这里用英语学习,你觉得什么容易? 什么难?

对当前英语的认知

12）在肯塔基大学学习了一段时间以后,你现在觉得自己的英语能力如何? 有什么改进?

13）在学业上,你是如何克服英语方面的挑战的?

14）这些是你的 QRI 分数,你如何看待这些分数,以及你如何看待你现在的表现?

15）你认为这些分数能反映你的实际英语能力吗?

16）是什么让你觉得对英语(学习或者使用)更舒适自如了?

17）你会做什么事情(抑或做了哪些事情)让自己持续学习英语?

18）你觉得真实的英语环境对你的英语学习有帮助吗?

19）关于你的英语学习,你还有什么想和我分享的吗?

7. 逐字转录采访录音并删除任何可能导致识别参与者或组织的措辞。访谈记录将为数据分析提供记录。

References

Abelmann, N., & Kang, J. (2014). A fraught exchange? U. S. media on Chinese international undergraduates and the American. *University Journal of Studies in International Education, 18*(4), 382-397.

Adler, P. S. (2006). International students in English-speaking universities. *Journal of Research in International Education, 5*(2), 131-154.

Allen, K. D., & Hancock, T. E. (2008). Reading comprehension improvement with individualized cognitive profiles and metacognition. *Literacy Research and Instruction, 47*, 124-139.

Almasi, J. F., & Fullerton, S. K. (2012). *Teaching strategic processes in reading* (2nd ed.). The Guilford Press.

Anderson, R. C., & Pearson, P. D. (1984). A schema-theoretical view of basic processes in reading. In P. D. Pearson (Ed.), *Handbook of reading research* (Vol.1, pp. 185-224). Longman.

Apel, K., & Masterson, J. (2001). *Beyond baby talk: From sounds to sentences: A parent's guide to language development.* Prima.

Au, K. H. (1997). A sociocultural model of reading instruction: The Kamehameha Elementary Education Program. In S. A. Stahl & D. A. Hayes (Eds.), *Instructional models in reading* (pp. 181-202). Erlbaum.

August, D., Francis, D. J., Hsu, H. A., & Snow, C. E. (2006). Assessing reading comprehension in bilinguals. *The Elementary School Journal, 107* (2), 221-238.

Bader, L. A., & Pearce, D. L. (2013). *Bader reading and language inventory* (7th ed.). Pearson Education.

Bailey, F., & Fransky, K. (2014). *Memory at work in the classroom*: *Strategies to help underachieving students.* ASCD.

Barton, D., & Hamilton, M. (1998). *Local literacies*: *Reading and writing in one community.* Routledge.

Bernhardt, E. (2005). Progress and procrastination in second language reading. *Annual Review of Applied Linguistics, 25,* 133-150.

Bernstein, B. (1972a). A sociolinguistic approach to socialization, with some reference to educability. In J. Gumperez & D. Hymes (Eds.), *Directions in sociolinguistics* (pp. 465-497). Holt, Rinehart & Winston.

Bernstein, B. (1972b). Social class, language, and socialization. In P. Giglioli (Ed.), *Language and social context* (pp. 157-178). Penguin Books.

Bourdieu, P. (1991). *Language & symbolic power* (Trans. G. Raymond & M. Adamson). Harvard University Press.

Bowen, G. A. (2008). Naturalistic inquiry and the saturation concept: A research note. *Qualitative research, 8*(1), 137-152.

Bronfenbrenner, U. (1979). *The ecology of human development*: *Experiments by nature and design.* Harvard University Press.

Brown, A. (1994). The advancement of learning. *Educational Researcher, 23* (8), 4-12.

Brown-Chidsey, R., Davis, L. & Maya, C. (2003). Sources of variance in curriculum-based measures of silent reading. *Psychology in the Schools, 40,* 363-377.

Brown, J.I., Fishco, V.V. & Hanna, G. (1993). *The Nelson-Denny reading test.* Riverside.

Brozo, W. G., & Afflerbach, P. P. (2011). *Adolescent literacy inventory, grades 6-12.* Allyn & Bacon/Pearson.

Bryman, A. (2016). *Social research methods* (5th ed.). Oxford University Press.

Calderón, M., Slavin, R., & Sánchez, M. (2011). Effective instruction for English learners. *The Future of Children*, *21*(1), 103-127.

Castillo-Montoya, M. (2016). Preparing for interview research: The interview protocol refinement framework. *The Qualitative Report*, *21*(5), 811-831.

Chang, T. (1939). A Chinese philosopher's theory of knowledge. *The Yen Ching Journal of Social Studies*, *1*(2), 164-171.

Ching, Y., Renes, S. L., McMurrow, S., Simpson, J., & Strange, A. T. (2017). Challenges facing Chinese international students studying in the United States. *Educational Research and Review*, *12*(8), 473-482.

Chu, T. K. (2004). 150 years of Chinese students in America. *Harvard China Review*, *5*(1), 7-26.

Cloud, N., Genessee, F., & Hamayan, E. (2000). *Literacy instruction for English language learners*: *A teacher's guide to research-based practice.* Heinemann.

Cobb, J. B., & Kallus, M. K. (2011). *Historical, theoretical, and sociological foundations of reading in the United States.* Pearson.

Coleman, C., Lindstrom, J.H., Nelson, J., Lindstrom, W. & Gregg, N. (2008*). Passageless comprehension of the Nelson-Denny reading test*: *Well above chance for university students.* Paper presented at the 15th Annual Meeting of Society for the Scientific Study of Reading, Asheville, NC.

Conley, M. W. (2008). *Content area literacy*: *Learners in context* (2nd ed.).

Allyn & Bacon.

Cooper, G. (1998). *Research into cognitive load theory and instructional design at UNSW.* University of New South Wales.

Creswell, J. W. (2009). *Research design: Qualitative, quantitative, and mixed methods approaches* (3rd ed.). Sage.

Curry, M. J. (2004). UCLA community college review: Academic literacy for English language learners. *Community College Review, 32*(2), 51-68.

Davies, N. F. (1976). Receptive versus productive skills in foreign language learning. *The Modern Language Journal, 60*(8), 440-443.

de Jong, P. F., & der Leij, A. V. (2003). Development changes in the manifestation of a phonological deficit in dyslexic children learning to read a regular orthography. *Journal of Educational Psychology, 95*, 22-40.

Denzin, N. K., & Lincoln, Y. S. (2005). Introduction: The discipline and practice of qualitative research. In N. K. Denzin & Y. S. Lincoln (Eds.), *The Sage handbook of qualitative research* (pp. 1-32). Sage.

Diaz, D. (2018). *Improving literacy in adult ELLs through metacognitive strategies for reading comprehension and academic achievement* (Doctoral dissertation). Northcentral University, San Diego, California.

Duke, N., & Carlisle, J. (2011). The development of comprehension. In M. L. Kamil, P. D. Pearson, E. B. Moje, & P. P. Afflerbach (Eds.). *Handbook of reading research* (Vol. IV) (pp. 199-228). Routledge.

Duke, N., Pearson, P., Strachan, S., & Billman, A. (2011). Essential elements of fostering and teaching reading comprehension. In S. J. Samuels & A. E. Farstrup (Eds.), *What research has to say about reading instruction* (4th ed., pp. 51-93). International Reading Association.

Ellis, R. (2015). *Understanding second language acquisition* (2nd ed.). Oxford

University Press.

ETS (2017). *Linking TOEFL iBT scores and IELTS scores*: *A research report*. ETS.

Everatt, J. (1997). The abilities and disabilities associated with adult developmental dyslexia. *Journal of Research in Reading*, *20*, 13-21.

Fang, Z., & Coatoam, S. (2013). Disciplinary literacy: What you want to know about it. *Journal of Adolescent & Adult Literacy*, *56*(8), 627-632.

Fang, Z., & Pace, B. G. (2013). Teaching with challenging texts in the disciplines: Text complexity and close reading. *Journal of Adolescent & Adult Literacy*, *57*(2), 104-108.

Feast, V. (2002). The impact of IELTS scores on performance at university. *International Education Journal*, *3*(4), 70-85.

Ferris, D. (2009). *Teaching college writing to diverse student populations*. The University of Michigan Press.

Fischer, K. (2012). *Many foreign students find themselves friendless in the U.S., study finds*. The Chronicle of Higher Education. http://www.lexisnexis.com/hottopics/lnacademic/.

Ford, R. (2020). Understanding SEVP: What to do if a student loses their F-1 status. https://fordmurraylaw.com/understanding-sevp-student-loses-f-1-status/.

Fu, Y., Machado, C., & Weng, Z. (2018). Factors influencing Chinese international students' strategic language learning at ten universities in the U.S.: A mixed-method study. *Journal of International Students*, *8*(4), 1891-1913.

Galstyan. (2020). F-1 student visa privileges and limitations. http://www.galstyanlaw.com/visas/students/f-1-privileges-and-limitations/.

Gareis, E. (2012). Intercultural friendship: Effects of home and host region. *Journal of International and Intercultural Communication*, *5*, 309-328.

Grabe, W. (2009). *Reading in a second language*: *Moving from theory to practice.* Cambridge University Press.

Graham, S. W., Donaldson, J. F., Kasworm, D., & Dirkx, J. (2000). *The experience of adult undergraduate students—What shapes their learning?* Paper presented at the Annual Meeting of the American Educational Research Association, New Orleans, LA. https://files. eric. ed. gov/fulltext/ ED440275.pdf.

Green, T. M. (2020). *The Creek & Latin roots of English* (6th ed.). Rowman & Littlefield Publishers.

Gubrium, J. F., & Holstein, J. A. (2003). *Handbook of interview research*: *Context and method.* Sage.

Gunning, T. G. (2010). *Creating literacy instruction for all children* (7th ed.). Allyn & Bacon.

Halliday, M. A. K. (1975). *Learning how to mean*: *Explorations in the development of language.* Arnold.

Hardy, C., & Tolhurst, F. (2014). Epistemological beliefs and cultural diversity matters in management education and learning: A critical review and future directions. *Academy of Management Learning & Education*, *13*(2), 265-289.

Heath, S. B., & Mangiola, L. (1991). *Children of promise*: *Literate activity in linguistically and culturally diverse classrooms.* National Education Association.

Hendricks, K. M. (2013). *Reading and test taking in college English as a second language students* (Doctoral dissertation). Syracuse University.

Hesse-Biber, S. N., & Leavy, P. (2011). *The practice of social research* (2nd ed.). Sage.

Hidi, S. (2001). Interest, reading, and learning: Theoretical and practical considerations. *Educational Psychology Review*, *13*(3), 191-209.

Hill, J. D., and Kathleen, M. F. (2006). *Classroom instruction that works with English language learners.* Association of Supervision and Curriculum Development.

Hock, M. F., Brasseur-Hock, I. F., & Deshler, D. D. (2015). Reading comprehension instruction for middle and high school students in English language arts: Research and evidence-based practices. In *Improving reading comprehension of middle and high school students* (pp. 99-118). Springer International Publishing.

Hofer, B. K. & Pintrich, P. R. (1997). The development of epistemological theories: Beliefs about knowledge and knowing and their relation to learning. *Review of Educational Research, 67*(1), 88-140.

Huang, Y. (2012). Transitioning challenges faced by Chinese graduates. *Adult Learn, 23*(3), 138-147.

IELTS (2001). *International English language testing system handbook*, joint publication of UCLES, the British Council and IDP Education Australia: IELTS Australia.

Institute of International Education (2019). *Open doors report on international educational exchange.* http://www.iie.org/opendoors.

International Association for the Evaluation of Educational Achievement (2001). *Progress in international reading literacy study.* IAEEA.

International Center of University of Kentucky (2019). *International student enrollment.* https://international.uky.edu/About/Enrollment.

Ip, D., Chui, E., & Johnson, H. (2009). *Learning experiences and outcomes of culturally and linguistically diverse students at the University of Queensland: A preliminary study.* The University of Queensland.

Jiang, X. (2011). The role of first language literacy and second language

proficiency in second language reading comprehension. *The Reading Matrix, 11*(2), 177-190.

Kaufman, J. (2004). The interplay between social and cultural determinants of school effort and success: An investigation of Chinese-immigrant and second-generation Chinese students' perceptions toward school. *Social Science Quarterly, 85*(5), 1275-1298.

Keenan, J. M. & Betjemann, R. S. (2006). Comprehending the Gray Oral Reading Test without reading it: Why comprehension tests should not include passage- independent items. *Scientific Studies of Reading, 10*(4), 363-380.

Kendeou, P., Muis, K. R., & Fulton, S. (2011). Reader and text factors in reading comprehension processes. *Journal of Research in Reading, 34*(4), 365-383.

Kern, R. G. (1988). *Foreign language reading: Linguistic, cognitive, and affective factors which influence comprehension.* ERIC.

Kobayashi, M. (2002). Cloze tests revisited: Exploring item characteristics with special attention to scoring methods. *Modern Language Journal, 86*(4), 571-586.

Koda, K. (2007). Reading and language learning: Crosslinguistic constraints on second language reading development. *Language Learning, 57*(1), 1-44.

Krashen, S. (1981). *Second language acquisition and second language learning.* Pergamon.

Krashen, S. (1985). *The input hypothesis: Issues and implications.* Longman.

Laplante, B. (1997). Teaching science to language minority students in elementary classrooms. *New York State Association for Bilingual Education Journal, 12*, 62-83.

Larsen-Freeman, D., & Cameron, L. (2008). *Complex systems and applied *linguistics*. Oxford University Press.

Laws, G., Brown, H. & Main, E. (2016). Reading comprehension in children with Down syndrome. *Reading and Writing*, *29*(1), 21-45.

Lei, S. A., Berger, A. M., Allen, B. M. Plummer, C. V., & Rosenberg, W. (2010). Strategies for improving reading skills among ELL college students. *Reading Improvement*, *47*(2), 92-104.

Leider, C. M., Proctor, C. P., Silverman, R. D. & Harring, J. R. (2013). Examining the role of vocabulary depth, cross-linguistic transfer, and types of reading measures on the reading comprehension of Latino bilinguals in elementary school. *Reading and Writing*, *26*(9), 1459-1485.

Leikin, M. & Assayag Bouskila, O. (2004). Expression of syntactic complexity in sentence comprehension: A comparison between dyslexic and regular readers. *Reading and Writing*: *An Interdisciplinary Journal*, *17*(7-8), 801-822.

Leslie, L., & Caldwell, J. S. (2017). *Qualitative reading inventory* (6th ed.). Pearson.

Lewis-Beck, M., Bryman, A., & Liao, T. (2004). *The Sage encyclopedia of social science research methods*. Sage.

Li, G., Chen, W., & Duanmu, J. (2010). Determinants of international students' academic performance: A comparison between Chinese and other international students. *Journal of Studies in International Education*, *14*(4), 389-405.

Li, H., & Suen, H. K. (2015). How do Chinese ESL learners recognize English words during a reading test? A comparison with romance-language-speaking ESL learners. *International Multilingual Research Journal*, *9*, 93-107.

Li, S., & Munby, H. (1996). Meta-cognitive strategies in second language academic reading: A qualitative investigation. *English for Specific Purposes*,

15(3), 199-216.

Liu, D. (2016). Strategies to promote Chinese international students' school performance: Resolving the challenges in American higher education. *Asian-Pacific Journal of Second and Foreign Language Education, 1*(8), 1-15.

Liu, J. (2016). How does studying aboard change Chinese students' choices of reading strategies? *The Canadian Modern Language Review, 72*(1), 40-65.

Longcope, P. (2009). Differences between the EFL and the ESL language learning contexts. *Views on Language and Culture, 30*(2), 303-320.

Matthiessen, S. J. (2011). *Essential words for the TOEFL: Test of English as a foreign language* (5th ed). Barron's Educational Series, Inc.

McClure, J. W. (2007). International graduates' cross-cultural adjustment: Experiences, coping strategies, and suggested programmatic responses. *Teaching in Higher Education, 12*(2), 199-217.

Merriam, S. (1998). *Qualitative research and case study applications in education.* Jossey-Bass.

Mezirow, J. (1997). Transformative learning: Theory to practice. *New Directions for Adult & Continuing Education, 74*, 5-8.

Mihara, K. (2011). Effects of pre-reading strategies on EFL/ESL reading comprehension. *TESL Canada Journal, 28*(2), 51-73.

Miles, M. B., Huberman, A. M., & Saldaña, J. (2014). *Qualitative data analysis: A methods sourcebook* (3rd ed.). Sage.

Miller, S. D., & Smith, D. E. P. (1984, May). *Differences in literal and inferential comprehension after reading orally and silently.* Paper presented at the 29th Annual Meeting of the International Reading Association, Atlanta, GA.

Miller, M., & Veatch, N. (2010). Teaching literacy in context: Choosing and using instructional strategies. *The Reading Teacher*, *64*(3), 154-165.

Moje, E. B. (2008). Responsive literacy teaching in the secondary school content areas. In M. W. Conley, J. R. Freidhoff, M. B. Sherry, & S. F. Tuckey (Eds.), *Meeting the challenge of adolescent literacy*: *Research we have research we need* (pp. 58-87). The Guilford Press.

Mokhtari, K., & Niederhauser, D. S. (2013). Vocabulary and syntactic knowledge factors in 5th grade students' reading comprehension. *International Electronic Journal of Elementary Education*, *5*(2), 157-170.

Murphy, P. K. & Mason, L. (2006). Changing knowledge and changing beliefs. In P. A. Alexander & P. Winne (Eds.), *Handbook of educational psychology* (pp. 305-324). Lawrence Erlbaum Associates.

Murphy, M., & Fleming, T. (2000). Between common and college knowledge: Exploring the boundaries between adult and higher education. *Studies in Continuing Education*, *22*(1), 77-93.

Nag, S. (2017). *Assessment of literacy and foundational learning in developing countries*: *Final report*. Health and Education Advice and Resource Team, Department for International Development (DFID). https://assets.publishing. service.gov.uk/media/593e6e6240f0b63e0b000249/Nag_ Final_Report_20170517. pdf.

Nardi, P. M. (2006). *Doing survey research*: *A guide to quantitative methods* (2nd ed.). Allyn & Bacon.

National Center for Educational Statistics (2001). *The national assessment of educational progress.* Institute of Education Sciences, US Department of Education.

National Center for Education Statistics (2003). *Literacy in everyday life*: *Results from the 2003 national assessment of adult literacy.* Institute of

Education Sciences.

Neeley, S. D. (2005). *Academic literacy* (2nd ed.). Pearson Education, Inc.

Nicholson, H. D. (2018). *Middle school educators' best practices for integrating technology in education: A descriptive case study* (Doctoral dissertation). University of Phoenix.

Nilsson, N. L. (2008). A critical analysis of eight informal reading inventories. *The Reading Teacher, 61*(7), 526-536.

Nisbett, R. E. (2003). *The geography of thought: How Asians and Westerners think differently...and why.* The Free Press.

O' Connor, H., & Madge, C. (2016). *Internet based interviewing.* University of Leicester. Chapter.

Organisation for Economic Cooperation and Development (2001). *Programme for international student assessment.* OECD Publications.

Ozuru, Y., Dempsey, K., & McNamara, D. S. (2009). Prior knowledge, reading skill, and text cohesion in the comprehension of science texts. *Learning and Instruction, 19*(3), 228-242.

RAND Reading Study Group & Snow, C. (2002). *Reading for understanding: Towards an R&D program in reading comprehension.* Rand Corporation.

Paris, S. G., & Carpenter, R. D. (2003). FAQs about IRIs. *The Reading Teacher, 56*(6), 578-580.

Perez, D., & Holmes, M. (2010). Ensuring academic literacy for ELL students. *American Secondary Education, 38*(2), 32-43.

Perry. K. (2012). What is Literacy? –A critical overview of sociocultural perspectives. *Journal of Language and Literacy Education [Online], 8*(1), 50-71.

Pikulski, J. J., & Chard, D. J. (2005). Fluency: Bridge between decoding and reading comprehension. *The Reading Teacher*, 58, 510-519.

Read, J. (2015). Defining and assessing academic literacy. In: *Assessing English proficiency for university study*. Palgrave Macmillan.

Ren, Z. (2006). *A cross-cultural study of epistemological beliefs and moral reasoning between American and Chinese college students* (Doctoral dissertation). Old Dominion University, Norfolk, VA.

Roe, B. R., & Burns, P. C. (2011). *Informal reading inventory*: *Preprimer to twelfth grade* (8th ed.). Wadsworth Cengage Learning.

Ross, K. M. (2017). IELTS vs. TOEFL: What are the differences? *US News*. https://www. usnews. com/education/best-colleges/articles/2017-02-16/ielts-vs-toefl-what-are-the-differences.

Ross-Gordon, J. M. (2003). Adult learners in the classroom. *New Directions for Students Services*, *102*, 43-52.

Ruiz, N. G. (2014). The geography of foreign students in U. S. higher education: Origins and destinations. *Brookings*. http://www. brookings. edu/research/interactives/2014/geography-of-foreign- students#/M10420.

Sawir, E. (2005). Language difficulties of international students in Australia: The effects of prior learning experience. *International Education Journal*, *6*(5), 567-580.

Sawir, E., Marginson, S., Deumert, A., Nyland, C., & Ramia, G. (2008). Loneliness and international students: An Australian study. *Journal and Studies in International Education*, *12*(2), 148-180.

Scarcella, R. & Oxford, R. (1992). *The tapestry of language learning*: *The individual in the communicative classroom*. Heinle & Heinle.

Schoenbach, R., Greenleaf, C., & Murphy, L. (2012). *Reading for understanding*: *How reading apprenticeship improves disciplinary learning in secondary and college classrooms* (2nd ed.). Jossey-Bass.

Schommer, M. (1990). Effects of beliefs about the nature of knowledge on comprehension. *Journal of Educational Psychology, 82*(3), 498-504.

Schommer, M. (1994). Synthesising epistemological beliefs research: Tentative understandings and provocative confusions. *Educational Psychology Review, 6*, 293-319.

Selinker, L. (1972). Interlanguage. *International Review of Applied Linguistics, 10*, 209-241.

Shanahan, C., Shanahan, T., & Misischia, C. (2011). Analysis of expert readers in three disciplines: History, mathematics, and chemistry. *Journal of Literacy Research, 43*(4), 393-429.

Sherry, M., Thomas, P., & Chui, W. H. (2010). International students: A vulnerable student population. *Higher Education, 60*(1), 33-46.

Shin, J., Deno, S.L. & Espin, C. (2000). Technical adequacy of the maze task for curriculum-based measurement of reading growth. *Journal of Special Education, 34*(3), 164-172.

Short, D., & Fitzsimmons, S. (2007). *Double the work*: *Challenges and solutions acquiring language and academic literacy for adolescent English language.* Report to Carnegie Corporation of New York. Alliance.

Simple Citizen (2020). *What are the privileges and limitations of a J1 visa?* https://learn. simplecitizen. com/immigration-support/privileges-limitations-j1-visa/.

Smith, L. (2007). Foreign students still face hurdles. *Chronicle of Higher Education, 53*(45), 31-41.

Snow, C. (2002). *Reading for understanding*: *Toward an R&D program in reading comprehension.* RAND.

Snow, C. E., Burns, S. M., & Griffin, P. (1998). *Preventing reading difficulties in young children.* National Academy Press.

Snow, C. E., & Sweet, A. P. (2003). Reading for Comprehension. In A. P. Sweet, & C. E. Snow (Eds.), *Rethinking Reading Comprehension.* The Guilford Press.

Stebleton, M. J. (2011). Understanding immigrant college students: Applying a development ecology framework to the practice of academic advising. *NACADA Journal, 31*(1), 42-54.

Suido, S. M., Shaunessy, E., Michalowski, J., & Shaffer, E. S. (2008). Coping strategies of high school students in an international baccalaureate program. *Psychology in the Schools, 45*, 960-977.

Sun, M. (2011). Experimental study of Chinese non-English students' overall learning style preferences. *US-China Education Review, A*(3), 346-354.

Taub, G. E., & Benson, N. (2013). Identifying the effects of specific CHC factors on college students' reading comprehension. *International Journal for the Scholarship of Teaching and Learning, 7*(2), 1-13.

Temple, C., Ogle, D., Crawford, A., & Freppon, P. (2011). *All children read:* *Teaching for literacy in today's diverse classrooms* (3rd ed.). Pearson.

Thorndike, R. L., (1973). Reading as reasoning: A study of mistakes in paragraph reading. *Journal of Educational Psychology, 8*, 323-332.

Torgesen, J. K., Wagner, R. K., Rashotte, C. A., Burgess, S., & Hecht, S. (1997). Contributions of phonological awareness and rapid automatic naming ability to the growth of word reading skills in second to fifth grade children. *Scientific Studies of Reading, 1*, 161-185.

Tracey, D. H., & Morrow, L. M. (2012). *Lenses on reading: An introduction to theories and models* (2nd ed.). The Guilford Press.

Tracy, S. J. (2013). *Qualitative research methods: Collecting evidence, crafting analysis, communicating impact.* Wiley-Blackwell.

Tweed, R. G., & Lehman, D. R. (2002). Learning considered within a cultural context. *American Psychologist, 57*(2), 89-99.

Uccelli, P., Phillips Galloway, E., Barr, C. D., Meneses, A., & Dobbs, C. L. (2015). Beyond vocabulary: Exploring cross-disciplinary academic-language proficiency and its association with reading comprehension. *Reading Research Quarterly, 50*(3), 337-356.

U.S. Department of State Travel (2020). *Study & Exchange.* https://travel.state. gov/content/travel/en/us-visas/study.html.

van Rijnsoever, F. J. (2017). (I Can't Get No) Saturation: A simulation and guidelines for sample sizes in qualitative research. *Plos One, 12*(7): e0181689.

Vankeer, H., & Vanderlinde, R. (2010). The impact of cross-age peer tutoring on third and sixth graders' reading strategy awareness, and reading comprehension. *Middle Grades Research Journal, 51*(1), 33-45.

Visa Guide World (2020). *US M-1 student visa.* https://visaguide.world/us- visa/ nonimmigrant/study-exchange-visas/m1/.

Vygotsky, L. (1978). *Mind in society.* MIT Press.

Vygotsky, L. (1986). *Thought and language.* MIT Press.

Wang, M. (2016). The impact of cultural values on Chinese students in American higher education. *The Qualitative Report, 21*(4), 611-628.

Wang, M., & Koda, K. (2005). Commonalities and differences in word identification skills among English second language learners. *Language Learning, 55*(1), 73-100.

Wang, Y. (2003). *The contextual knowledge of language and culture in education*: *Exploring the American university experiences of Chinese graduate students* (Doctoral dissertation). http://aquila. usm. edu/theses_dissertations/2631/.

Wang. Y. (2019). Expanding meaningfulness: Perceptions and strategy use of Chinese international graduate students in disciplinary reading. *Journal of International Students, 9*(2), 661-681.

Weideman, A. (2007). *Academic literacy*: *Prepare to learn* (2nd ed.). Van Schaik.

Weideman, A. (2018). Academic literacy: Why is it important? [Introduction.] *Academic literacy*: *Five new tests.* Geronimo Distribution.

Wiederholt, J. L., & Bryant, B. R. (1992). *Gray oral reading test* (3rd ed.). PRO-ED.

Wiederholt, J. L., & Bryant, B. R. (2001). *GORT 4*: *Gray oral reading tests examiner's manual.* PRO-ED.

Wiley, H. I. & Deno, S. L. (2005). Oral reading and maze measures as predictors of success for English learners on a state standards assessment. *Remedial and Special Education, 26*(4), 207-214.

Williams, R. S., Ari, O., & Santamaria, C. N. (2011). Measuring college students ' reading comprehension ability using cloze tests. *Journal of Research in Reading, 34*(2), 215-231.

Woolfolk, A. E. (1998). *Educational psychology* (7th ed.). Allyn & Bacon.

Wrigley, H. S., Chen, J., White, S., & Soroui, J. (2009). Assessing the literacy skills of adult immigrants and adult English language learners. *New Direction for Adult and Continuing Education, 121*, 5-24.

Xue, M. (2013). Effects of group work on English communicative competence of Chinese international graduates in United States institutions of higher education. *The Qualitative Report, 18*(7), 1-19.

Yamashita, J. (2003). Processes of taking a gap-filling test: Comparison of skilled and less skilled EFL readers. *Language Testing, 20*(3), 267-293.

Yan, K., & Berliner, D. C. (2009). Chinese international students' academic stressors in the United States. *College Student Journal, 43*(4), 939-960.

Yeh, C. J., & Inose, M. (2003). International students' reported English fluency, social support satisfaction, and social connectedness as predictors of acculturative stress. *Counseling Psychology Quarterly, 16*(1), 15-28.

Yin, R. K. (2009). *Case study research: Design and methods* (4th ed.). Sage.

Yin, R. K. (2014). *Case study research: Design and methods* (5th ed.). Sage.

Zhang-Wu, Q. (2018). Chinese international students' experiences in American higher education institutes: A critical review of the literature. *Journal of International Students, 8*(2), 1173-1197.

Zhang, Z. (1992). *The effects of teaching reading strategies on improving reading comprehension for ESL learners.* Paper presented at the Annual Meeting of the Mid-South Educational Research Association, Knoxville, TN.

Zhao, Y., Jindal-Snape, D., Topping, K., & Todman, J. (2008). Theoretical models of culture shock and adaptation in international students in higher education. *Studies in Higher Education, 33*(1), 63-75.

Zhou, Z., Peverly, S. T., Xin, T., Huang, A. S., & Wang, W. (2003). School adjustment of first-generation Chinese-American adolescents. *Psychology in the Schools, 40*(1), 71-84.

Zuilkowski, S. S., Piper, B., Kwayumba, D., & Dubeck, M. (2019). Examing options for reading comprehension assessment in international contexts. *Journal of Research in Reading, 42*(3-4), 583-599.